Giovanna Magi

PARIS

A COMPLETE GUIDE
TO THE CITY

13 Itineraries with Detailed Maps
260 Colour Photographs
Street Map of Paris
Layouts of the Louvre and the Musée d'Orsay

VERSAILLES - THE PALACE AND GARDENS

BONECHI

© Copyright by Casa Editrice Bonechi - Via dei Cairoli 18b - Firenze - Italia
Phone + 39 055 576841 - Fax + 39 055 5000766
E-mail: bonechi@bonechi.it - Internet: www.bonechi.it

Publication created and designed by Casa Editrice Bonechi
Graphic design and cover: Manuela Ranfagni
Page-making: Laura Settesoldi
Editing: Simonetta Giorgi and Paula Boomsliter
Drawings: Stefano Benini and Fiorella Cipolletta

Texts and picture research: Giovanna Magi

Printed in Italy by Centro Stampa Editoriale Bonechi

ISBN 88-476-0667-5

* * *

The Thousand Faces of Paris

Who doesn't remember Ernest Hemingway's lauds of the festive spirit of Paris, or his praise of how the city inspires eating, drinking, writing, and love-making? It was 1921, but even today, as we watch a new millennium unfold, millions of people who have who have chosen this city as a travel destination are sharing the sensations of that young, impoverished American.

But which Paris? Just how many Paris' are there? There's tourist Paris, the city of the great monuments of the past; there's the unavowed, unsung Paris of the minor museums and hidden corners; there's the Paris of shopping and fashion; there's culinary Paris; there is the Paris of the banks of the Seine and of the great parks.

Or might it not be that there's just one Paris, with a thousand faces, ever-changing, with a million facets, a city that has remained true to itself through the centuries and is always renewing itself? Charles Baudelaire wrote that Paris changes 'faster than do our hearts', and its evolution does indeed resemble more a revolution than a slow process of change.

Paris has been sung, filmed, painted, danced, painted, and written.

Whispered in the haunting, hurting treble of Edith Piaf or in Aznavour's hoarse tenor, evoked by the feline movements of the 'Black Venus' Joséphine Baker, conjured in the melancholy notes of Yves Montand and Gilbert Bécaud, traced in the dance steps of Mistinguette and Chevalier, for whom 'Paris sera toujours Paris'.

Paris is 'blue and lazy', Paris is a 'scoundrel and a rogue', Paris is applauded and damned, hell and lover.

The favourite subject of an entire generation of painters who set to canvas the city's face and its colours, protagonist on the silvers screen of stories of mystery and of romance, asylum for political exiles, for scientists in search of glory, for persecuted poets, for ill-omened artists. A gilded exile for those revelling in society life and for those searching for silence and oblivion.
Thomas Jefferson, before he became president of that nation which, like France would only a few years later, had learned how to fight and to be free, defined Paris a 'second home'.
Millions of words have been written about Paris - by those who have seen her and those who have dreamed her, by those who have lived here and those who have only imagined doing so. In each of these souls, Paris has left a mark - of culture, of love, of wealth, of simple and all-encompassing *joie de vivre*.

'Je t'aime, ô capitale infâme!'
(Charles Baudelaire)

THE FRENCH ROYAL DYNASTIES

MEROVINGIAN
from Clovis I
(481-511)
through
Childeric III
(743-761)

CAROLINGIAN
from Pépin III
'le Bref'
(751-768)
through Louis V
(986-987)

CAPETIAN
from Hugues
Capet
(987-996)
through
Charles IV
(1322-1328)

VALOIS
from
Philippe VI
(1368)
through
Henri III
(1574-1589)

BOURBON
from Henri IV
(1589-1610) through
Louis-Philippe I
(1830-1848)

A BRIEF HISTORY OF THE CITY

Allegory of the City of Paris on the façade of the Hôtel de Ville.

*P*aris was probably founded by the Gauls, who built a small settlement on the left bank of the Seine. The city is mentioned, with the name of Lutetia, by Julius Caesar who came here in 53 BC
As a result of the continual menace of the barbarian invasions, this original settlement was moved to the île de la Cité, and from there it expanded along the banks of the river. The residence first of the Merovingian and then of the Carolingian kings, Paris became a real capital in 987, when Hugues 'Capet', the first Capetian king, founded a new and powerful dynasty. One of Paris' moments of maximum splendour was between 1180 and 1223, when Philippe II Auguste came to the throne: the construction of the Louvre was begun and the University was founded. During the reign of Louis IX 'le Pieux' (Saint Louis, 1226-1230), the Sainte-Chapelle was built and work on the Notre-Dame cathedral was continued. But the next dynasty, that of the Valois kings, brought wars and catastrophe, disorder and civil discord to Paris.

Although Charles V briefly restored order, the fighting between the Armagnacs and Burgundians became more and more savage: this led to the occupation of France by England, and in 1430 Henry VI was crowned king of France.

In 1437, Charles VII reconquered Paris, but the population was exhausted by the bloody revolts alternating with epidemics of the plague. Although throughout the 16th century the kings preferred to live in the castles of the Loire rather than in the capital, this did not end the internecine struggles in Paris itself. The spread of the Protestant religion created discord which for a long time rent Paris and the whole of France, culminating in the massacre of the Huguenots on the infamous night of St Bartholomew (24 August 1572). After Henri III had been assassinated in 1589, the city was besieged for four long years until finally it opened its gates to Henri IV, who had converted to Catholicism.

At the beginning of the 17th century, however, Paris already had no less than 30,000 inhabitants. The city became more and more important under the powerful Cardinal Richelieu and during the new dynasty of the Bourbon kings: at the time of Louis XIV, the Sun King, it had half a million inhabitants.

But Paris earned its real place in history after 1789, the year of the French Revolution, which was to mark the birth of the modern world. The long years of terror, in which many lives were lost and irreparable damage was done to so many works of art, were forgotten in the splendour of the Empire and the dazzling court created by Napoleon, crowned emperor in 1804.

From 1804 to 1814, Paris was constantly being enriched: the Arch of Triumph was built, the Vendôme column erected, and the Louvre enlarged. After the fall of the monarchies of Charles X and Louis-Philippe Bourbon-Orléans, the Second Republic was born and then Napoleon III took the throne. He entrusted the task of replanning the city to Baron Haussmann: the markets of Les Halles were

Joan of Arc meeting Charles VII at Loches.

Paris and the Seine in the 1600s.

Portrait of Louis XIV.

Napoleon III and Baron Haussmann.

built, the Bois de Vincennes and Bois de Boulogne laid out, the Opéra erected, and the great boulevards, typical expression of this historical era, were opened up.

The year 1871 marked a new and sad page in the history of Paris with the Commune (18 March - 28 May). Many splendid historic buildings were lost in these days of rebellion and destruction by fire: among others, the Hôtel de la Ville and the palace of the Tuileries. But Paris had new moments of splendour at the beginning of the 20th century, with the World Exhibitions, the construction of the Grand Palais and the Petit Palais, and the birth of important movements of art, painting and literature. Unfortunately the city had yet to suffer the bombardments and destruction of two long wars. During World War II it fell into the hands of the German Army in 1940 and was not liberated by the Allies until 1944. But from that moment until today, as a city finally alive and free, Paris has resumed its place in the history of culture and humanity.

PARIS AND THE REVOLUTION

*A*lmost all of the French Revolution was played out in Paris; it was here that the most significant events of the period took place.

It all began in the gardens of the Palais-Royal on 12 July 1789, when a passionate speech by Camille Desmoulins fired the populace, already infuriated and oppressed by a deepening economic crisis, and highly critical of the Crown, whose style of government it no longer tolerated.

The trees of the garden provided the revolutionaries with the first green leaves, the colour of hope, from which they fashioned their cockades. Two days later the Bastille - symbol of absolute monarchy - was stormed, taken, and demolished.

After the last, humiliating visit of the king to Paris, on 17 July, control of the situation passed once and for all into the hands of the Jacobins and the Cordeliers, the able organizers of the expedition of 5 and 6 October that brought the royal family back to the Tuileries from Versailles. Flanking Louis XVI was now the

Camille Desmoulins haranguing the crowd at the Palais-Royal on 12 July 1789.

6

National Constituent Assembly, which on 2 November nationalized the lands of the clergy.

The king lived in the Tuileries for 34 months, exception made for his shameful escape as far as Varennes in June 1791. Then, the revolutionaries' doggedness, plus the king's abiding weakness and indecision and the subtle and well-simulated double-cross perpetrated by the queen, brought the situation to a head: the rulers were moved to the tower of the Temple, where they remained imprisoned from 13 August 1792 until their separate executions by the guillotine, in Place de la Révolution. Unfortunately, both the Tuileries and the Temple, the last two dwelling-places of a king incapable of reacting to events, were ravaged and destroyed.

The taking of the Bastille.

Spared, instead, was much of the 'antechamber' to the guillotine, the Conciergerie, where prisoners awaited their turn to board the wagon that would carry

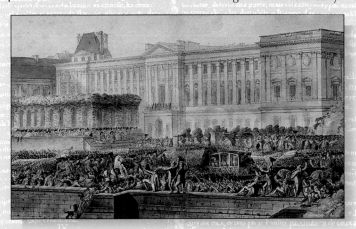

The king arriving at the Hôtel de Ville on 17 July 1789.

them to their place of execution.

The final destination of this historical itinerary constellated by dramatic events was the Place de la Révolution, today's Place de la Concorde, theatre to the last acts in the lives of so many of the figures that made the history of Paris and indeed of all of France, from Louis XVI to Marie-Antoinette, from Charlotte Corday to Lavoisier, from Danton to Robespierre - nor must we forget Madame Roland, who, just before she was guillotined, addressing the statue of Liberty set in place of the statue of Louis XV, uttered the famous words, 'O Liberty, what crimes are committed in thy name!' One thousand one hundred heads fell under the blade of the guillotine in the span of thirteen months. Altogether, the victims of the French Revolution were 60,000.

Bistrots and brasseries in Paris

The Parisian bistrot was born in the 19th century, on occasion of an event of such extraordinary importance as the extensive work by the architect Haussmann, and came to its full flower during the World Fair celebrating the arrival of the 20th century and which took as its symbol par excellence the 'dame de fer'- the incredible Eiffel Tower. In the years of Paris' face-lift (that is, when Baron George Haussmann, as Prefect of the Seine, organised and directed massive restructuring of a large part of the urban fabric of the capital, literally changing its face between 1853 and 1870 - and incidentally thus creating a point of reference for all the metropolises of the modern world), both the London-style *restaurants* and their rivals the plain, welcoming, lively, and utilitarian bistrots arose and achieved popularity and notoriety. The first attracted the upper middle class and the aristocracy of France; the second the workers, the students - and in general people who couldn't spend much money, or who indeed had very little *to* spend. Although theoretically these two extraordinary types of meeting-places could have cancelled each other out, in Paris instead both sur-

vived, even though today they have both in part lost their original functions, for the very simple reason that implacable Time has since changed society. In their heyday, and actually until not very long ago (the last authentic bistrots may be said to have closed when the old Les Halles market was torn down), the daily menu at the bistrots was strictly linked to the 'laws' of the neighbourhood markets: every day a specialty, a featured dish. Just as in the beginning, when from the country, and in particular from the Central Massif, the wine and charcoal merchants came to Paris and opened the cafés, the public-houses, the bistrots, and shops selling wine or fuel. These were the famous *bougnats* where one drank but could also find something plain, but most importantly, hot, to eat. Thus, in the complicated and fascinating 19th century, initiatives of this type blossomed all over Paris, all similar but with different names: the *troquets*, the *bistroquets*, the *bouillons*, the *crèmeries*, the *brasseries*, and many neighbourhood taverns.

What has remained of this extraordinary tradition? In Paris, quite a bit, even if the genuineness of old has somewhat suffered. Does this means that in the bistrots and brasseries of Paris or of Lyon one no longer eats as well? Absolutely not; in fact, quite the contrary. Today, famous chefs snobbily define their restaurants as bistrots, even though they seem to forget the appellation when they add up the bill. But be that as it may, today these are extraordinary eating-places that have been relaunched by extraordinary people who believe in what they are doing and usually do it very well. One example is 'Lipp' in the St-Germain quarter, which reminds us that it was originally created by a *porteur d'eau* in the years of Paris' transformation: the founder was one of the many who came from the country bringing wine, fuel, firewood, and fresh drinking water to the capital.

A chef like Guy Savoy, from the school of Troisgros, runs a superlative restaurant in Rue Troyon, but he also manages six bistrots. And he has written a book of recipes for the dishes served ... not at the restaurant, but in the bistrots!

What should one order in these eating-places? Lentils, veal tongue *en gribiche*, fricassee of porcini mushrooms, the remarkable *magret de canard au poivre*, the terrine of pigs' trotters, Morteau sausages, salami *en croûte de brioche*, extraordinary salt-and fresh-water fish, the *blanquette de veau*, sweetbreads, liver, kidneys, the *cassoulet*, tripe, calf's head, tails, and any number of desserts, like *pain perdu* or the *Tarte Tatin*.

Today, which of the bistrots are best known and most highly regarded by the Parisians themselves - even though they make some inevitable concessions to the tourist palate? Although it is difficult to choose, we might mention Chez Georges at no. 1 Rue du Mail, Le Bourguignon du Marais at no. 52 Rue François Miron, Chez Catherine at no. 65 Rue de Provence, Au Petit Boileau at no. 98 Rue Boileau, Le Baratin at no. 3 Rue Jouye-Rouvé, Chez Michel at no. 10 Rue de Belzunce, Caves Pétrissans at no. 30 Avenue Niel, and scores of others disseminated throughout all the different quarters of Paris. It's great fun to try to pick them out for yourself - and almost always, the prize is a great meal!

(Piero Paoli)

We would like to offer a 'tasty' suggestion to all those visitors to Paris who are a little unsure of how to order the renowned creations of the French cuisine from the menu of a restaurant, brasserie, or bistrot.
Here's a list of what we feel are some of the best known and easiest to find of these wonderful dishes.

Amuse-gueule: appetizers of various types, served at the start of a meal.

Andouillettes: chopped sausages.

Blanquette de veau: cut-up veal shank cooked in broth with mushrooms, onion, and parsley.

Bouillabaisse: rich fish soup served over toasted bread with garlic and hot pepper sauce.

Bûche de Noël: log-shaped pastry with coffee cream filling.

Cailles aux raisins: sautéed quails roasted with grapes.

Canard à l'orange: braised duck served with an orange-and-lemon sauce.

Cassoulet: stewed pork with vegetables, onion, sausage, and beans

Charcuterie: cold cuts.

Choucroute: sauerkraut cooked in white wine and pork broth, served with smoked pork and sausages.

Civet de lièvre: salmi of hare.

Coq au vin: cut-up chicken sautéed with bacon, garlic, and mushrooms and casseroled with Burgundy wine.

Côtes de veau: veal cutlets sautéed in butter and served with various sauces.

Crêpes Suzette: French pancakes in a sauce of jam and orange juice, flamed with liqueurs.

Croque-monsieur: toasted ham-and-cheese sandwiches on white bread.

Crudités: raw vegetables served as appetizers.

Dinde aux cèpes: stuffed turkey served with mushrooms.

Entrecôte: roast sirloin of beef, served with sauce.

Escargots à la bourguignonne: snails cooked in their shells with garlic, butter, and parsley.

Estouffade: different meats, fried and then cooked in broth with onions and wine.

Gigot d'agneau: roast lamb 'larded' with slivers of garlic.

Grenouilles: frogs

Hachis: different chopped meats served with vegetables and various sauces.

Homard à l'Armoricaine: Northern lobster sautéed with onion, tomatoes, white wine, and brandy.

Homard Thermidor: Northern lobster cut lengthwise and grilled with a mustard cream sauce topping.

Huîtres: oysters.

Île flottante: Floating Island dessert - poached meringues on custard.

Langouste à la Parisienne: boiled spiny lobster cut into rounds, with artichokes and hard-boiled eggs in aspic.

Lapin en gibelotte: braised rabbit with onions, mushrooms, and white wine.

Magret de canard: filleted duck breasts in sauce prepared with blood.

Parmentier: chopped meat with mashed potatoes, au gratin.

Quiche Lorraine: ham-and-custard pie.

Rillettes: potted goose and pork, served cold.

Ris de veau: baked sweetbreads.

Soupe à l'oignon: French onion soup made with chicken broth and Port wine, sprinkled with Parmesan cheese, and browned in the oven.

Suprême de volaille: boiled chicken breasts served with various sauces.

Tarte Tatin: a thin pastry crust with caramelized apples, served upside-down.

Tournedos: grilled fillet of beef.

A page dedicated to Parisian cuisine is, to say the least, de rigueur in any guide to the monuments and artistic sites of Paris. From the infinite variety of dishes offered by French cuisine, we have selected four that may be defined as being 'historical' in all senses.

*B*oiled Hen à la Henri IV - This is a one-dish meal, to be followed by cheese and a dessert, takes it name from the son-in-law of Catherine de' Medici and husband of Marguerite de Valois (Queen Margot), who proclaimed that the table of every French family would be graced with a chicken every Sunday.

*T*arte Tatin - The story behind this most famous of French *tartes* runs thus: while cooking in her small hotel, Fanny Tatin inadvertently turned her apple pie upside down as she put it in the oven. A disaster? Quite the contrary - and when it came to the ears - or the palate - of the pastry chef at Maxim's, he lost no time in

making it a star item on the menu.

*B*ouillabaisse - Frédéric Mistral, the great Provençal poet awarded the Nobel Prize for Literature in 1904, defined this dish as 'the soup of gold'. Its name derives from the Provençal *bouiabaisso*, in turn a contraction of the verbs for 'boil' and 'reduce'. Legend has it that one day Saint Peter in person, in the guise of a beggar, knocked at a poor woman's door, asking for something to eat. The woman had only a glass of wine and some fish her son had caught, and unsure of how to prepare the food, she asked the beggar's help. Saint Peter thus showed her the recipe for what is today considered one of the best fish stews in the world.

*L*obster 'Armoricaine' - This is a *chef d'oeuvre* of luxury French dining. We know that the dish was invented in Paris in the 19th century by a French chef who, however, came from the United States. His recipe encountered such success that it is still featured on the menus of the great classical-style restaurants.

The Charm of the Marchés aux Puces

*W*hat's more fun than shopping in Paris? You can find literally everything in the shops of the capital: Faubourg, St Honoré, Avenue Montaigne, the Champs-Élysées, Place Vendôme - the only problem is choosing, if what you're looking for are refined, luxury objects in refined, luxuriant settings.

But there's shopping and shopping: if your predilection is for finding the unfindable, Paris's flea markets, authentic paradises for collectors, are the place to go.

Maybe you won't strike the bargain of your life. Maybe you won't find a Van Gogh under a 'crust' or a genuine Louis XIV for only a few thousand francs. What is certain is that you'll have the time of your life exploring that labyrinth of stands and tiny shops where window-shopping, picking over goods, and arguing and bargaining are the order of the day.

Paris offers the visitor a number of such treasure troves, among which the best known is probably the flea market of Saint-Ouen, at the gates of Clignancourt, which in truth is formed of a number of smaller markets - covered and open-air - each with its own specialization: Biron, Vernaison, Serpette, Paul Bert, Rosier, Jules Vallès. You can also strike a good bargain at the Puce de Montreuil, called the 'thieves' market' by Parisians, and the Puce de Vanves in the 14th arrondissement.

The important thing is to get there early, very early, on Saturday morning, wherever you go. Plan to already be there when the *brocanteurs* start setting out their wares: this is the moment to get something at the best price.

Good buys are certainly not lacking - and however the haggling goes, in any case you will bring home a little piece of history, which - as we well know - breathes life into every single object, no matter how small or apparently insignificant.

INDEX OF ITINERARIES

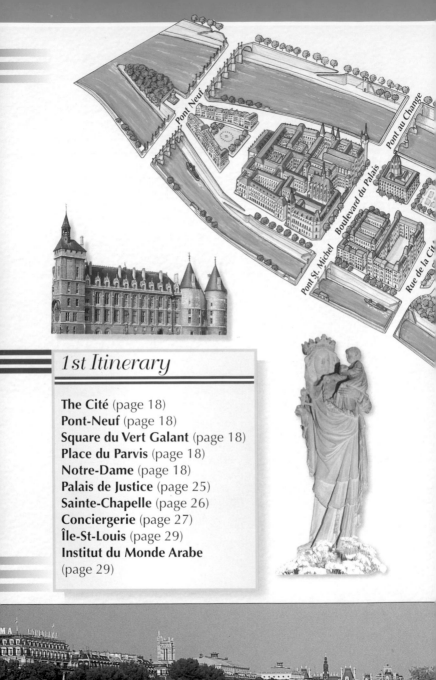

1st Itinerary

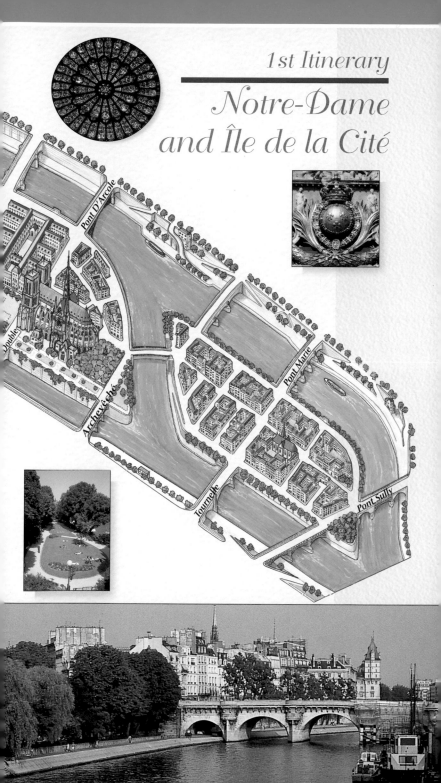

Notre-Đame
and Île de la Cité

Pont D'Arcole

Doubley

Archevêché

Pont Marie

Tournelle

Pont Sully

THE CITÉ – Centre of the city's life since the 3rd century, the Cité was founded on what was the largest of the islands in the Seine. It was the first settlement and first religious centre, and here were erected the Cathedral and the Palais de Justice. Numerous bridges link it to the banks of the Seine, along which run the picturesque *quais*. One of the most animated and colourful of the quays is the **Quai de Montebello,** extending between the bridges called Pont de l'Archevêché and Pont au Double: it is full of life and its parapets are lined with the typical *bouquinistes*, the sellers of rare and strange books and prints old and new.

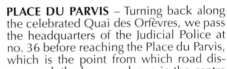

PONT-NEUF AND SQUARE DU VERT GALANT – Walking along the Quai St Michel and the Quai des Grands-Augustins, we reach this bridge, which is the oldest in Paris, planned by Du Cerceau and Des Illes. Begun in 1578 under Henri III and completed under Henri IV in 1606, it has two slender round arches and in the middle the **equestrian statue of Henri IV**. The square is reached by a stairway behind the statue of the king. It is the furthermost point of the Cité and one of the most beautiful parts of Paris.

Statue of Henri IV.

PLACE DU PARVIS – Turning back along the celebrated Quai des Orfèvres, we pass the headquarters of the Judicial Police at no. 36 before reaching the Place du Parvis, which is the point from which road distances in France are measured: the bronze plaque in the centre of the square in front of the cathedral indicates the starting point for all the nation's roads. On the north side of the square stands the grandiose **Hôtel-Dieu,** a hospice founded in the 7th century but rebuilt between 1868 and 1878; on the west side is the **Palais de la Préfecture de Police.** Overlooking the square is the imposing Notre-Dame, the cathedral of Paris.

NOTRE-DAME

The cathedral of Notre-Dame stands on the site of a Christian basilica which had in turn been built on the site of a temple from the Roman era. Its construction was begun in 1163, under Bishop Maurice de Sully: first the chancel was built, followed over the years by the nave and aisles and the façade, completed by Bishop Eudes de Sully in about 1200, the towers being finished in 1245. The architects Jean de Chelles and Pierre de Montreuil then constructed the chapels in the aisles and in the chancel. Towards 1250, the façade of the north arm of the transept was also completed; the other, that of the south arm, was not begun until eight years later. The church could be said to have been completed in 1345. In 1793 it ran the risk of being demolished; at this time, during the French Revolution, it was dedicated to the goddess of Reason. Reconsecrated in 1802, it was the scene two years later of the coronation of Napoleon I by Pope Pius VII. It was restored by Viollet-le-Duc between 1844 and 1864.

FAÇADE – It is divided vertically into three parts by pilasters and horizontally into three areas by its two galleries; in the lowest zone are the three portals. Above the portals runs the **Gallery of the Kings,** with its 28 statues representing the kings of Israel and Judea. In 1793 the people, seeing them as the hated French kings, knocked them down, but they were later put back in place. The central zone of the façade contains two great mullioned windows, on either side of a rose window measuring about 10 metres in diameter (1220-1225). In the centre are the *statues of the Virgin and Child with Angels,* on either side *Adam* and *Eve.* Above this part is a gallery of closely-set carved arches which link the two towers at the sides; though never completed, the towers contain splendid, extremely high two-light windows. Viollet-le-Duc filled this uppermost zone with gargoyles, grotesque figures with strange and fantastic forms, projecting from pinnacles, spires, and extensions of the walls.

The façade of Notre-Dame.

Detail of one of Notre-Dame's gargoyles.

Central portal. On this is depicted the *Last Judgment.* On the pier which divides it in two is the *statue of Christ,* while in the embrasures there are panels with the *personifications of the Vices and Virtues* and *statues of the Apostles.* Around the curve of the arch are the *Heavenly Court, Paradise,* and *Hell.* The lunette containing the *Last Judgment* is divided into three parts, dominated by the figure of Christ flanked by the Virgin, St John, and angels with the symbols of the Passion. Below are the *Blessed* on one side and the *Damned* on the other. In the lower part, the *Resurrection.*

Right portal. Also called the Portal of St Anne, it dates from 1160-1170, with reliefs from the 12th and 13th centuries. On the dividing pier, a *statue of St Marcel.* In the lunette, the *Virgin between Two Angels* and at the sides *Bishop Maurice de Sully* and *King Louis XII.*

Left portal. Also called the Portal of the Virgin, it is the finest of the three. On the dividing pier, the *Virgin and Child,* a modern work. In the lunette above, the *Death, Glorification, and Assumption of the Virgin.* On the door-posts are depicted the *Months of the Year,* in the embrasures figures of saints and angels.

RIGHT SIDE – On this side of the church is the *Portal of St Stephen,* begun by Jean de Chelles in 1258 and completed by Pierre de Montreuil, with its splendid large rose window and another smaller one in the cusp. Here can be seen the **spire,** soaring above the centre

The exquisite Gothic decoration of the front portals of Notre-Dame. The gallery with the 28 statues of the kings of Israel and Judea runs under the rose window.

20

of the cathedral, 90 metres high: it was rebuilt by Viollet-le-Duc, who depicted himself among the *Apostles* and *Evangelists* which decorate it.

INTERIOR – Its dimensions are impressive: 130 metres long, 50 metres wide and 35 metres high, it can contain up to 9,000 persons. The interior is divided into a nave and four aisles by cylindrical piers each 5 metres in diameter, with a double ambulatory around the transept and chancel. The **rose window** in the façade, above the 18th-century organ, depicts the *Signs of the Zodiac*, the *Months* and the *Vices and Virtues*. Above the arcades runs a gallery with double openings, surmounted in turn by ample windows. The **chapels** following one after the other up to the transept have a wealth of works of art from the 17th and 18th centuries: outstanding are two paintings by Le Brun, the *Martyrdom of St Stephen* and the *Martyrdom of St Andrew*, in the first and second chapels on the right respectively. The two ends of the transept have splendid stained-glass windows from the 13th century. The one in the north transept

Two details of the sculptural decoration.

A nocturnal view of the cathedral.

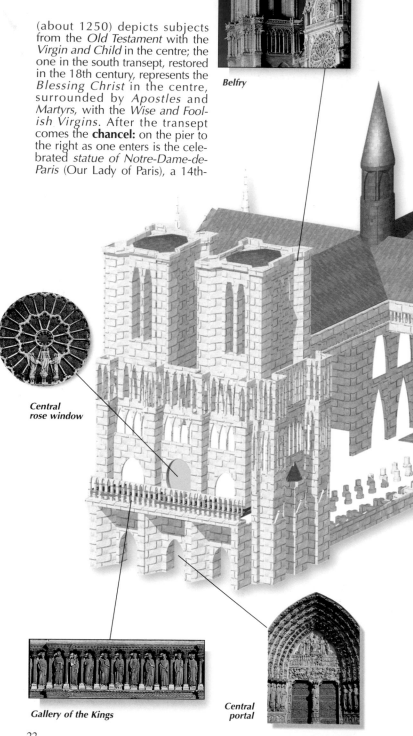

(about 1250) depicts subjects from the *Old Testament* with the *Virgin and Child* in the centre; the one in the south transept, restored in the 18th century, represents the *Blessing Christ* in the centre, surrounded by *Apostles* and *Martyrs*, with the *Wise and Foolish Virgins*. After the transept comes the **chancel:** on the pier to the right as one enters is the celebrated *statue of Notre-Dame-de-Paris* (Our Lady of Paris), a 14th-

Belfry

Central rose window

Gallery of the Kings

Central portal

century work once in the St-Aignan Chapel.
Around the chancel are carved wooden choir
stalls (18th century); on the high altar, a *statue
of the Pietà*, by Nicolas Coustou, in the
centre, with *Louis XIII* by Guillaume Coustou
and *Louis XI* by Coysevox at the sides. An
uncompleted marble chancel screen, decorated with reliefs (works by Jean Ravy and Jean
le Bouteiller), separates the
chancel from the
ambulatory,
and in the
radial

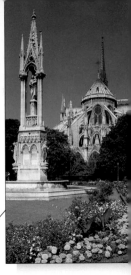

Apse

Southern rose window

chapels around it are
numerous tombs. On the
right, between the Chapelle
St-Denis and the Chapelle
St-Madeleine, is the
entrance to the **Treasury:**
it contains much sacred
silverware and important
relics, among them a fragment of the True Cross, the
Crown of Thorns, and the
Holy Nail.

Statue of Notre-Dame-de-Paris

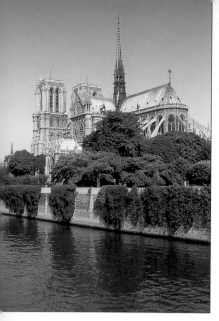

The right side and the apse of the cathedral.

APSE – This is one of the most daring apses of the Middle Ages, with flying buttresses 15 metres long, built by Jean Ravy (14th century).

Next to the apse of Notre-Dame is the **Square Jean XXIII:** its present appearance and its Neo-Gothic fountain date from a reorganisation project in 1844. We now walk along the **Quai aux Fleurs** and **Quai de la Corse,** where there is a picturesque and typical flower market every day, substituted on Sundays by an equally colourful bird market. Beyond the **Pont Notre-Dame,** we reach the headquarters of the **Tribunal de Commerce** and then the bridge called the **Pont au Change,** the name of which derives from the many moneychangers' shops concentrated here in the Middle Ages.

A Cathedral for the Big Screen and Beyond

In 1831, Victor Hugo immortalized Paris' cathedral in that which is generally considered one of his greatest works, *Notre Dame de Paris*. The beauty of the subject, the drama and the vividness of the characters were soon to conquer the world of celluloid as well. The two versions of *The Hunchback of Notre Dame*, one produced in 1923 and the other in 1939, were both were inspired by the touching figure of Quasimodo, the cripple with his deformed features who reacquires a semblance of happiness only at the sound of the six great bells. Two more movies on the same theme were produced in 1956 and 1982. In 1996, the Disney studios breathed life into a cartoon version of the novel, and two years later a successful musical version of the story debuted on the stage.

PALAIS DE JUSTICE

This is a huge complex of buildings, including the **Palais de Justice** itself, the **Sainte-Chapelle**, and the **Conciergerie**. On this same site the Roman rulers had their administrative and military headquarters; the kings of the Merovingian dynasty followed their example, and later the Capetians erected a chapel and a keep here. In the 13th century, Louis IX built the Sainte-Chapelle and in the following century Philippe IV 'le Bel' had the Conciergerie palace constructed. In 1358, after the bloody revolts of the Parisians headed by Étienne Marcel, Charles V decided to move his residence to the Louvre and leave the palace here to the Parliament, which used it to house the supreme court of justice of the kingdom. In later times, the buildings were repeatedly damaged by fires: in 1618 the Grande Salle was burnt, in 1630 the tall spire of the Sainte-Chapelle, in 1737 the Debtors' Court, and in 1776 the Galerie des Marchands. The judicial system, which until then had remained intact, was overturned by the Revolution. The new courts were established in the old building, which was given the name of Palais de Justice (Palace of Justice). Important works of restoration carried out under the direction of Viollet-le-Duc gave the building its present-day appearance. Facing the Boulevard du Palais is its monumental façade. On the right, the **Tour de l'Horloge,** or Clock Tower, dating from the 14th century. The clock dates from 1334, while the reliefs are by Germain Pilon (1585). After this comes the façade of the Civil Court, 14th-century in style though it was built in 1853. In the centre of the façade, a high wrought-iron gateway (1783-1785) leads into the **May Courtyard,** built in 1786 by Antoine and Desmaisons. From here, through a vaulted passageway on the left, one reaches the Sainte-Chapelle.

The façade of the Palace of Justice, with to the left the soaring spire of the Sainte-Chapelle.

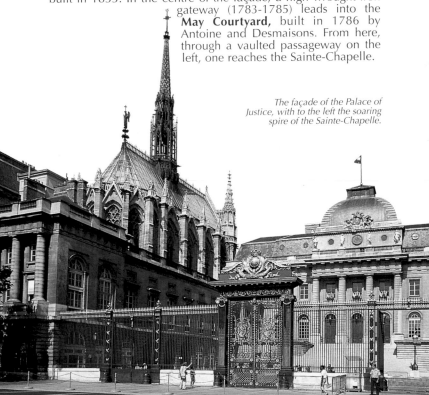

The interior of the Lower Church.

SAINTE-CHAPELLE

Built for Louis IX (Saint Louis) to contain the Crown of Thorns which the sovereign had bought in 1239 in Venice, it was designed by Pierre de Montreuil and consists of two chapels, one above the other, which were consecrated in 1248. Above its high base (which corresponds to the lower chapel), there are vast windows crowned with cusps. The steep sloping roof has a marble balustrade and a slender open-work spire 75 metres high. Two more towers with spires stand on each side of the façade, in front of which is a porch; above the porch is a great rose window with cusp (late 15th century), with themes from the Apocalypse.

Lower Church. Barely 7 metres high, it has an enormous nave compared with the two much narrower aisles at the sides. Trefoil arch motifs supported by slender shafts recur around the walls. The **apse** at the end is polygonal. The dominating note of the chapel is its extremely rich polychrome decoration.

The interior of the Upper Church, with its famous stained-glass windows.

Upper Church. It is reached by means of an internal staircase. Without aisles, it is 17 metres wide and 20.5 metres high. A high plinth, punctuated by open-work marble arcades which from time to time open onto deep niches, runs all around the church. In the third bay are the two niches reserved for the king and his family. On each pier is a 14th-century statue of an Apostle. All the architectural elements of the church are thus reduced to a minimum, so as to leave room for the fifteen huge *stained-glass windows,* 15 metres in height, which with their 1134 scenes cover a surface of some 618 square metres. They date from the 13th century and depict *Scenes from the New and Old Testaments* in vivid, glowing colours.

CONCIERGERIE

This severe building dates back to the time of Philippe le Bel, that is, to between the end of the 13th and the beginning of the 14th centuries. The name Conciergerie derives from *concierge,* the Royal governor who had charge of the building. Today it occupies the north wing of the Palais de Justice. From the Quai de la Mégisserie, the side of the building can be admired in all its beauty, with its twin towers: on the right the **Tour d'Argent,** where the Crown jewels were kept, and on the left the **Tour de César.** From the 16th century, the Conciergerie was a State prison: during the Revolution thousands and thousands of prisoners condemned to death were kept in its cells, including Marie-Antoinette, the king's sister Madame Elisabeth, Charlotte Corday, and the poet André Chenier.

> **INTERIOR** *(The entrance is at no. 1 Quai de l'Horloge)* – On the ground floor is the **Hall of the Guards,** with massive piers supporting Gothic vaults, and the huge **Hall of the Men-at-Arms.** The latter room, which has four aisles and is no less than 68 metres long, 27 metres wide, and 8 metres

The massive building that is the Conciergerie.

high, was once the dining-hall of the king. From the nearby kitchens, with four enormous fireplaces in the corners, banquets could be prepared for at least a thousand guests. In a large room with cross vaults, prisoners could have, for a certain fee, straw pallets on which to pass the night; in another area, with the tragically ironic name of *Rue de Paris,* the poor prisoners were quartered. The most evocative cell is without doubt the one occupied from 2 August to 16 October 1793 by Marie-Antoinette; it was converted into a chapel in 1816 by the only remaining daughter of Louis XVI, the Duchess of Angoulême. The cell now communicates with the one occupied first by Danton and later by Robespierre. From here one reaches the **Girondins' Chapel,** which was converted into a collective prison: here the crucifix of Marie-Antoinette is kept. From the chapel one reaches in turn the **Women's Courtyard**, used by the female prisoners.

The Execution of Marie-Antoinette

On 16 October 1793, the public prosecutor of the Revolutionary Tribunal of Paris, Fouquier-Tinville, read the sentence by which 'Marie-Antoinette of Austria, widow of Louis Capet' was condemned to death.

The last day of she who had been dubbed 'Madame Deficit' began at four in the morning, when - without a flicker of emotion - she had heard the judgment of conviction and had returned to her cell to prepare for her last journey. Her camisole and petticoat were black; her dressing-gown, *fichu*, and mousseline bonnet, white. Her wrists were bound behind her back.

Louis XVI had met his death inside a closed carriage, but this privilege was denied his wife. His queen, 'that Austrian', made her last journey seated alone on a dirty wagon, exposed to the insults and derisive shouts of the people that lined the streets leading to the place of her execution.

At a window along Rue St-Honoré was the painter Jacques Louis David; a few strokes of his pencil have left us an unforgettable and cruel portrait-caricature of Marie-Antoinette, sitting erect, her face an impenetrable mask, her lips set in a tight, disdainful line. That which had been one of her most endearing characteristics - the charming pout typical of all the Hapsburgs - had been transformed into an expression of dark and total contempt for everything that surrounded her.

This is the last official image we have of Marie-Antoinette: a broken and humiliated woman facing death with immense dignity. Her mortification was not to last long, however - Marie-Antoinette was guillotined at just 15 minutes past noon.

ÎLE ST-LOUIS

The entrance to the Institut du Monde Arabe. The exterior wall is decorated with the motifs typical of the musharabiya.

Returning to the top end of the Cité and crossing the modern Pont St-Louis, we reach the Île St-Louis, a place which retains its ancient fascination. Passing by the **Pont de la Tournelle,** originally built as a wooden bridge in 1370 but rebuilt several times and bearing a statue of *Ste Geneviève,* the patron saint of Paris, we reach the **Church of St-Louis-en-l'Île.** This was begun in 1664 to a design by Le Vau but completed only in 1726; the interior has three aisles and is a splendid Baroque creation, with a wealth of gold, enamel work, and polychrome marbles.

Coming out of the church, we pass the Pont Sully to reach the end of the island, occupied by the Square Henri IV, a tiny garden with the *monument to the sculptor A. L. Barye.* Continuing along the Quai d'Anjou, we find the island's finest mansions. At no. 2 is the **Hôtel Lambert,** built in 1640 by Le Vau and decorated by Le Brun and Le Sueur. At no. 17 is the entrance to the **Hôtel de Lauzun,** one of the most luxurious examples of a private 17th-century dwelling. It was built in 1657 to Le Vau's plans, and belonged to the Duke of Lauzun (from whom it took its name) for only three years. Théophile Gautier founded the 'Club des Haschischins' there and lived in the building with another great poet, Charles Baudelaire. Today the building belongs to the City of Paris, which uses it for important official guests. At no. 27 Quai d'Anjou is the residence of the Marquise de Lambert, who created a literary circle here. From this point we walk along the Quai de Bourbon to the other end of the island.

INSTITUT DU MONDE ARABE – Located on Rue des Fossés-Saint-Bernard at the corner of Pont Sully, this glass, aluminum, and cement creation by Jean Nouvel, Pierre Soria, and Gilbert Lezenes (1987) admirably succeeds in harmonizing modern needs with the purest Arab tradition in a light beautifully filtered by the typical motifs of the *musharabiya.*
The nine floors of the building, which covers an area of more than 26,000 square metres, host an important Arab culture documentation centre, a museum, a library, and ample exhibit spaces. The north side of the Institute building, opening on the Seine, reflects the façades of the palaces that line the Île-St-Louis.

2nd Itinerary

Practical Information for the Visitor

Louvre Museum (Métro: Line 1, Palais-Royal / Musée du Louvre station).
Hours: Open every day except Tuesday from 9:00 a.m. to 6:00 p.m. Late closing at 9:45 p.m. on Wednesday (entire museum) and Monday (short tour).
Main entrance from the Pyramid in the Cour Napoléon. Other entrances at Porte des Lions, Richelieu passage (groups), and Carrousel.

Information: Phone 01 - 40205151
Minitel 3615 Louvre
Internet www.louvre.fr

To avoid lines at the Pyramid, we suggest purchasing your tickets in advance by phone (0803808803) or via Minitel or Internet.

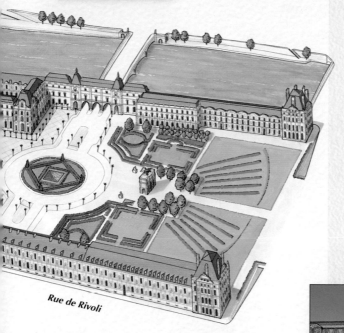

Rue de Rivoli

The Louvre castle as it appeared in the retablo of the Parliament of Paris (anonymous Flemish painter, mid-15th century).

Scale models of the Louvre (Munier and Polonovski, 1:1000 scale). The palace as it appeared in 1380 and, bottom, in 1870.

HISTORY

The origin of the Louvre goes back to the end of the 12th century, when Philippe II Auguste, before leaving for the Third Crusade, had a fortress built near the river to defend Paris from the incursions of the Saxons (in fact the name Louvre seems to derive from the Saxon word *leovar*, meaning 'fortified dwelling'): this original nucleus occupied about a quarter of the present-day Cour Carrée. The king continued to live on the Cité, so that the fortress was used to contain the Treasury and the archives. In the 14th century, Charles V, known as 'le Sage' (the Wise), decided to make it his residence and had the famous Library constructed. But the kings did not live in the Louvre again until 1536, when François I, after having the old fortress knocked down, erected on its foundations a palace more in keeping with Renaissance tastes. Work proceeded under Henri II and Catherine de' Medici, who gave Philibert Delorme the task of constructing the Tuileries Palace and uniting it to the Louvre by means of a wing stretching out towards the Seine. The modifications and extensions to the palace continued under Henri IV, who had the Pavillon de Flore constructed, and under Louis XIII and Louis XIV, who completed the Cour Carrée and

had the western façade with the Colonnade erected. In 1682, when the royal court was transferred to Versailles, work was virtually abandoned and the palace fell into such a state of ruin that in 1750 its demolition was even contemplated. But work on the palace, suspended during the Revolution, was resumed by Napoleon I. His architects, Percier and Fontaine, began building the north wing, finished in 1852 by Napoleon III, who finally decided to complete the Louvre. During the period of the Commune, in May 1871, the Tuileries palace was burnt down and the Louvre assumed its present appearance. After the important Library of Charles the Wise had been dispersed, it was François I who, in the 16th century, first began an art collection. This was considerably enlarged under Louis XIII and Louis XIV, so much so that by the death of the latter the Louvre was already used regularly for exhibitions of paintings and sculptures. On 10 August 1793, it was opened to the public and its gallery thus finally became a museum. From then on, the collection was continually enlarged: Napoleon I went so far as to demand a tribute in works of art from the nations he conquered. The objects listed in the museum's catalogue today are subdivided into seven sections: from ancient Egyptian, Greek, Etruscan, and Roman to Oriental works, from medieval to modern sculpture, and from the objets d'art such as those belonging to the Royal Treasury to the immense collections of paintings.

THE MUSEUM

The starting point of the 'Grand Louvre' project was the decision made by the President of the Republic Mitterrand, in 1981, to restore the Louvre palace to its former function as a museum, and the first step was to move the Ministry of Finance, then based in the Flora Pavilion, to Bercy. Furthermore, in order to increase the exhibition area and connect the Louvre and the city more closely, new spaces were created under the

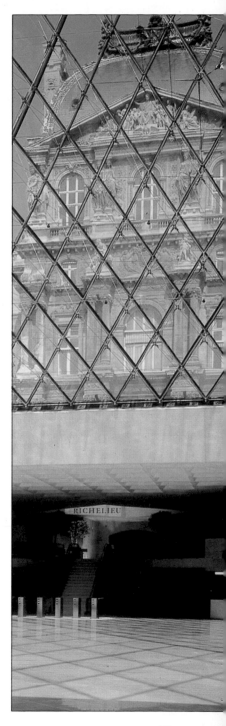

View of the Richelieu Pavilion from inside the large Pyramid.

The Louvre Pyramids by Ieoh Ming Pei, at night.

Greek art: Venus de Milo.

Cour Napoléon. The link between the new rooms and the ground above is the magnificent light structure of the glass pyramid, flanked by three smaller pyramids that, as does the larger one, reflect the changing light of the Parisian sky in their transparency. The author of this daring project, which has been the cause of much discussion both by Parisians and others, is Ieoh Ming Pei, an American architect of Chinese origin who was already responsible for the construction of the new wing of the National Gallery in Washington.

The definitive transformation of the Louvre from palace to museum took place on 18 November 1993, two hundred years after the Louvre was first opened to the public, with the inauguration of the Richelieu Wing.

The Richelieu Wing, with its 6 collections distributed in 22,000 square metres divided into 165 rooms, on four floors, can be said

to be the new face of the Louvre, characterised by a new reading of the works of art and by a different kind of pleasure given by the exhibition spaces.

The reorganisation of the Richelieu Wing has also involved the modification of what were the old Ministry of Finance car parks. Thanks to the wonderful transformation of the two courts and the fact that they have been covered (with a superb glass structure 30 metres tall), all the monumental statues of the French school created for outdoors (squares, parks and public gardens) can be exhibited here. These two courts, the Cour Puget and the Cour Marly (1800 square metres the first; 2150 the second) have kept their original side entrance, so that it is possible to look down into them from the Richelieu Passage even if one is simply passing by.

A description of the total renovation of the museum (transformations in the Denon Wing and in the Sully Wing from 1993 through 2001) must include the Carrousel Passage. It was designed by the architects Michel Macary

Leonardo da Vinci, Mona Lisa.

Egyptian art: Seated Scribe.

and Gérard Grandval and is characterised by a central upside down pyramid, also the work of Pei, which lights the underground space and creates a sort of logical continuity with the Napoléon Hall. The windows of many shops (fashion, cosmetics, perfume, jewellery, records, books) face onto these vast galleries which converge on the pyramid. There are also banks, restaurants, a post office, the Museum Bookshop, and the CyberLouvre.

From this space it is possible to see the remains of the ancient Louvre of the Capetian era, built by Philippe II Auguste as a fortress, in the centre of which was an impressive round keep, 30 metres high and surrounded by a deep ditch. The truncated cone which formed the base (diameter 15 metres, height 7 metres), is in an excellent state of preservation.

In the light of all these new modifications and changes, the Louvre museum is divided into the following 7 departments: **Oriental Antiquities and Islamic Art; Egyptian Antiquities; Greek, Etruscan, and Roman Antiquities; Objets d'art; Sculpture; Graphic Arts; Paintings.**

VISIT TO THE COLLECTIONS

Oriental Antiquities and Islamic Art: Richelieu Wing (mezzanine and ground floor) and Sully Wing (ground floor).

Egyptian Antiquities: Sully Wing (mezzanine, ground floor and first floor) and Denon Wing (mezzanine).

Greek, Etruscan and Roman Antiquities: Denon Wing (ground floor) and Sully Wing (ground floor and first floor).

Objets d'art: Richelieu Wing (first floor, where the *Apartments of Napoleon III* are also to be found: open to the public for the first time, they are a perfect and rare decorative unity from the Second Empire); Sully Wing (first floor) and Denon Wing (first floor).

Sculpture: Richelieu Wing (mezzanine and ground floor) and Denon Wing (mezzanine and ground floor).

Pictures: Richelieu Wing (second floor, French pictures from the 14th to the 17th century and Dutch, Flemish, and German pictures); Sully Wing (second floor, French pictures from the 17th to 19th century) and Denon Wing (first floor, large-size 19th-century French pictures and Italian and Spanish pictures).

Graphic Arts: Richelieu Wing (second floor, Northern schools); Sully Wing (second floor, French school) and Denon Wing (first floor, Italian school).

Mediaeval Louvre

These departments are arranged in three wings that are reached by means of an escalator from the Napoléon Hall under the large pyramid: the **Richelieu Wing.** which runs along Rue de Rivoli; the **Denon Wing.** which runs parallel to the Seine; the **Sully Wing,** which runs round the Cour Carrée. In order to visit all the various collections, the visitor is invited to follow the routes marked in different colours on the plans on page 37.
The mezzanine of the Sully Wing with the **Mediaeval Louvre** and the History of the Louvre must also be added to these exhibition spaces.
Thanks to the new Richelieu Wing, it has been possible to allow certain large cycle of works the right exhibition space, above all the 24 paintings dedicated to the life of Marie de' Medici, commissioned from Rubens by the Queen of France in 1622: unveiled in 1625, they were initially conceived for the west

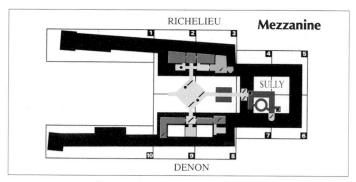

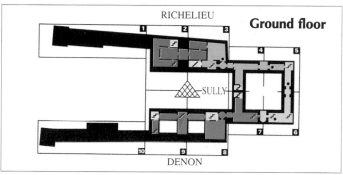

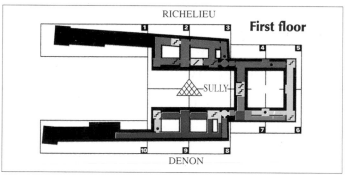

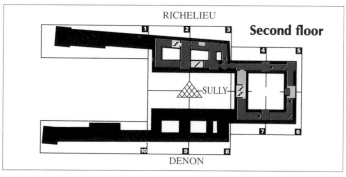

gallery of the Luxembourg Palace. The **Medici Gallery** which holds them today is a vast space of 524 square metres, covered by a barrel vault and lit, as are the other rooms in this section, by zenithal light which caresses the pictures without ever striking them violently.

Prominence is also rightly given to another group of works, the **12 tapestries depicting the Hunts of Maximilian,** woven in Brussels around 1530 from designs by Bernard van Orley. Nor must the **Khorsabad Court** (Oriental Antiquities, Room 4) be forgotten. It is a splendid and exciting evocation of the Palace of King Sargon II at Dur Sharrukin, what is now the town of Khorsabad, near Mosul.

ORIENTAL ANTIQUITIES

The Oriental Antiquities section, set up in 1881, is rich in exhibits referred to the vast zone which stretches from Bosphorus to the Persian Gulf.

The neo-Sumerian statues, which stylistically continue the previous Akkad dynasty period, are important: of these, a group of around thirty specimens representing *Gudea,* the *patési* of the city of Lagash, a dignitary who held political and religious offices, stand out. The majority of these statues come from Tello, discovered during French excavations. One of the objects, beautiful in the simplicity of its conception, is the one bought by the Louvre in 1953: made from dolerite, it is 1.05 metres high and can be dated between 2290 and 2255 BC. In a praying position, with his hands together, Gudea wears the typical Persian lamb hat on his head and a simple cloak over his shoulders. From the Mari excavations comes a small *alabaster statue depicting the official Ebih-il,* sitting with his hands together on a wicker stool; such chairs are still used today in Iraq. Of extraordinary importance not only as a work of art, but also as a historical document, is the famous *Stela of Hammurabi* (beginning of the 2nd millennium): a block of black basalt, 2.25 metres high, with the 282 laws which made up the legislative regulations and customs of the ancient Sumerians inscribed in the Akkadian language: these laws influenced the Justinian and Napoleonic Codes. There is some extremely beautiful evidence of Assyrian strength between the 9th and 7th centuries BC: for instance, the decorations of the palaces of Nimrud, Nineveh, and Khorsabad, with the grandiose, four-metre-high *winged bulls* with human heads. The *archers* of the Emperor's private guard, the so-called Immortals, come from the magnificent palace of Darius at Susa: each one is 1.47 metres high and made of glazed and painted brick. Mesopotamia, in fact, had little stone and thus always used bricks baked in the sun and then

glazed. Finally, there are the antiquities from Palestine and the Syrian-Phoenician region up to its furthest points, Tunisia and Algeria.

Persian art: the Archers of Darius.

EGYPTIAN ANTIQUITIES

This universally famous department was founded by Jean-François Champollion, who first deciphered the hieroglyphics. The Egyptian section of the Louvre has been continually enriched by purchases and donations and now offers the widest documentation possible on the civilization which developed along the Nile, from its dawning to the Ptolemaic, Roman, and Byzantine periods.

The statuette of the *Seated Scribe* belongs to the Old Kingdom and was made during the 5th Dynasty, maybe around 2500 BC. Found at Saqqarah in 1921, the statuette, 53 centimetres high, is made of painted limestone and the eyes are encrusted with hard stones: the cornea in white quartz, the iris in rock crystal, and the pupils in ebony. Animated by an intense internal life, the scribe appears to interrogate with his eyes, ready to begin his work on the roll of papyrus resting on his lap. The Louvre possesses all the decorated part of the *Mastaba of Akhtibetep* (5th Dynasty), with scenes illustrating daily life, and the famous head of a man called *'Salt Head'* because of its severe expression. The *statue of the Chancellor Nakhti*, of surprising realism and with the wood still bearing traces of the original colour, and the harmonious *Girl Bearing Offerings*, in plastered wood, are from the Middle Kingdom (12th Dynasty). We should not forget the powerful naturalism of the works from the period of Akhenaton, the heretic pharaoh, such as his extraordinary *sandstone bust* discovered by Henri Chevrier or the *Princess' Head*, characterized by a very long neck.

An entire section has been dedicated to *Coptic art*, with a rich documentation of cloths, tapestries, detached frescoes, and architectural remains.

Egyptian art: the Vizier Seny-nefer and his wife Hatshepsut.

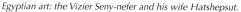

Egyptian art: painted limestone bas-relief with the pharaoh Seti I and the goddess Hathor.

The Egypt of the Roman era is documented above all in the form of funerary art from the first century BC through the fourth century AD. Don't miss the extraordinary series of exceptionally vivid and realistic portraits painted in wax on wooden panels, known as the *Fayyum Portraits*.

GREEK, ETRUSCAN, AND ROMAN ANTIQUITIES

Like the Egyptian one, this section offers an extraordinary panorama of artistic material from the archaic age to the late Roman Empire.
The masterpieces are so many and so famous that it is almost impossible to mention them all.
For the archaic period it is enough to remember the *Lady of Auxerre,* the *Hera of Samos,* and the discreet, ironic smile illuminating the face of the *Rampin Horseman.* The classical period is well represented by a fragment of the *Frieze of the Panathenaean Women,* from the Parthenon of the Acropolis at Athens: created in Phidias' workshop in the 5th century BC, it is also known as the *Frieze of the Ergastine Women.* Two sculptures have contributed to the fame of the museum which hosts them: the *Winged Victory of Samothrace* and the *Venus de Milo.* The former, found in 1863, is in Parian marble and perhaps commemorates the successes of the natives of Rhodes in the war against Antiochus III. The latter was discovered in 1820 by a peasant on the island of Melos in the Cyclades. It is dated around the end of the 2nd century BC. Although it certainly derives from a Praxiteles original, it has become the prototype of Greek female beauty. Roman art is represented, amongst others, by the *frieze from the Ara Pacis* in Rome (9 BC); a statue depict-

Greek art: head of the Rampin Horseman.

Greek art: the Victory of Samothrace.

ing *Augustus* (considered to be one of the finest portraits of the Emperor); a series of *portraits of Trajan, Hadrian, Antoninus Pius.* Apart from the bronzes, with the outstanding beauty of the *Apollo of Piombino,* there is the Greek-Roman jewellery, with the famous *Boscoreale Treasure,* found in a villa destroyed in 79 AD by the eruption of Vesuvius.

PAINTING COLLECTIONS

The collection of paintings at the Louvre is no doubt the best in the world and was started by François I (1515-1547). This sovereign began a true and proper collection of all types of works, destined to enrich the royal residence at Fontainebleau. He managed to secure the most famous artist of that time, Leonardo da Vinci, and thus the possession

Hubert Robert, The Louvre Gallery.

of some of his most important works, such as the *Mona Lisa* and the *Virgin of the Rocks.* A further impetus was given to the collections by Louis XIII, although the true collector was not the king but his minister, Cardinal Richelieu, who left everything to the Crown when he died. The collection was still relatively modest: an estimate made at the time numbered the paintings at 200. A real step forward came with the next king, Louis XIV, who bought part of Cardinal Mazarin's collection and the collection of Charles I of England. The collection grew further at the end of the 1700s, following requisitions from churches, noble families, or dissolved associations. Even though many works had been returned to their rightful owners by the end of 1815, from the Second Empire onwards a wise purchasing policy consented continual enrichment with works of ever increasing importance, thus constantly enlarging the collections.

THE FRENCH SCHOOL

The paintings of the French school are, naturally, the most numerous of the whole picture gallery.
Amongst the masterpieces there is the *Villeneuve-lès-Avignon Pietà,* an International Gothic masterpiece attributed to Enguerrand Quarton; the portraits include the *portrait of King Jean le Bon,* painted by an anonymous artist around 1360, and the splendid *portrait of Charles VII,* the '*très victorieux*' sovereign, painted by Jean Fouquet in 1444. The 16th century sees the

Fontainebleau School, Gabrielle d'Estrées and the Duchess of Villars.

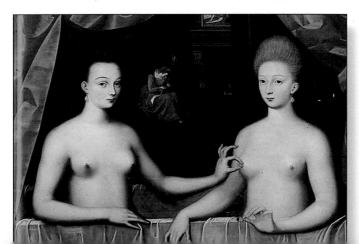

Jacques-Louis David, The Oath of the Horatii.

splendid art of Jean and François Clouet (the latter was court painter in 1540) and that of the Fontainebleau School, a very refined example of which is the painting depicting *Gabrielle d'Estrées and the Duchess of Villars.* The works of the three Le Nain brothers, Antoine, Louis, and Mathieu, are also very interesting: Louis is considered to be the best: far removed from the pomp of the court, he specialized in portraying rustic scenes such as the *Peasant Family,* painted around 1643. Of considerable interest is Georges de la Tour who, in his *St Joseph the Carpenter* and *Mary Magdalene with an Oil-lamp,* shows Caravaggian influences following a visit to Rome. The Roman lesson can also be seen in Nicolas Poussin's *Arcadian Shepherds* and *Rape of the Sabine Women* as well as Claude Lorraine's *Sea Port* and, above all, *Campo Vaccino in Rome,* which is full of the golden light typical of a sleepy afternoon at the Roman Forum. *Ex-Voto,* by Philippe de Champaigne, is in perfect agreement with the artist's Jansenist ideals; it was painted between 22nd January and 15th June 1662, to thank God for the miraculous healing of his paralysed daughter. In contrast with the serenity and mysticism of this composition is the opulence of the *Portrait of Chancellor Séguier,* painted by Charles Le Brun and clearly inspired by the models of the Italian 16th century.

Antoine Watteau most highly expressed Rococo: his *Embarkation for the Island of Kythera,* which was much discussed because of its difficult interpretation, should be remembered, as should the luminary *Gilles,* maybe painted around 1717 or 1719. The triumph of French Rococo was mainly due, however, to François Boucher, whose frequent descriptions of Venus were defined as 'Boudoir Venuses' (e.g., *Diana at Rest after Bathing*) and Jean-Honoré Fragonard, Boucher's pupil, with his sensual colours and full shapes (*The Bathers*). Then, in agreement with the enthusiasm and admiration for antiquity, there is the domination of Jacques-Louis David's neoclassicism: *The Oath of the Horatii,* a true and proper manifestation of the new pictorial creed, the *Portrait of Madame Récamier,* of great purity and acute psychological introspection, and the *Coronation of Napoleon I,* a huge, 54-square-metre painting that definitively consecrated the artist as the first painter of the new Empire. In spite of the strong 16th century influence, Pierre-Paul Prud'hon's *Transportation of Psyche* announces the themes used in Romanticism. Romanticism in fact explodes with Théodore Géricault who, inspired by a tragic and famous event (the shipwreck in 1816 of a French frigate carrying settlers to Senegal), painted the *Raft of the Medusa* in 1819, where the diagonal composition is just a tangled heap of disjointed bodies with hallucinated and dramatic faces. The work of the other great Romantic artist, Eugène Delacroix, should be placed next to that of Géricault. The museum possesses some of his greatest paintings, such as the famous *Liberty Guiding the People,* a true and

Théodore Géricault, The Raft of the Medusa.

proper manifestation of political propaganda, the *Death of Sardanapalus,* where the colours in the painting recall the artist's long stays in Spain and Morocco, and the *Conquest of Jerusalem by the Crusaders* and the *Women of Algiers.* These two artists are contrasted by Jean-Auguste Ingres who opposes their colours with the purity of his fine and sinuous lines and refined curves: just observe the *Grande Odalisque* or the *Turkish Bath,* the latter inspired by the description of a harem in Lady Montague's letters. The Louvre possesses over 130 paintings by another famous artist, Camille Corot. His *Woman with a Pearl,* painted in 1868 in the pose of the Mona Lisa, is almost a prototype for all of his portraits: a still and quiet drawing with a sense of calm and serenity characterizes all of his works, be they portraits or landscapes.

Eugène Delacroix, Liberty Guiding the People.

THE ITALIAN SCHOOL

Of all the foreign schools at the Louvre, the Italian one is without doubt the best represented, featuring some true and proper masterpieces. The best of Florentine painting is present with the solemn *Majesty* by Cimabue, who perpetuates the Byzantine inspiration with rigorous symmetry and steady gestures, as well as the *altar steps of St Francis* by Giotto. The 15th century is exalted by the *Coronation of the Virgin* by Fra' Angelico, an episode of the *Battle of San Romano* by Paolo Uccello, the pure *Portrait of a Princess of the House of Este* by Pisanello, and works by Antonello da Messina (*The Condottiere*) and Andrea Mantegna (a monumental *St Sebastian* and geometrical *Crucifixion*). The genius of Leonardo shines at the Louvre with three of his most beautiful works, which are famous throughout the world: *St Anne with the Virgin and Child and Lamb*, painted between 1506 and 1510 for the high altar of the Church of the Servites in Florence; the *Virgin of the Rocks*, mysterious and cleverly constructed; the *Mona Lisa*, painted between 1503 and 1505 and so loved by the artist

that he always took it with him until it was sold in France to François I, either by Leonardo himself or by Melzi. This painting was the prototype for Renaissance portrait-painting and became even more famous when it was stolen from the Salon Carré in 1911 and found two years later in Florence. Some other great Italian works are the *Belle Jardinière* and *Portrait of Baldassarre Castiglione* by Raphael, the *Woman at the Mirror, Open-air Concert*, and *The Entombment of Christ* by Titian, and *The Wedding at Cana* by Veronese, an enormous painting where the artist inserts a crowd of over one

Cimabue, Virgin in Glory.

Leonardo da Vinci, Virgin of the Rocks.

hundred people under a typically Palladian architecture. Also present are *Hunting* and *Fishing* by members of the Carracci family, Caravaggio's *Death of the Virgin,* of a great realism, and Francesco Guardi's series of paintings in honour of Alvise Mocenigo.

THE FLEMISH AND DUTCH SCHOOLS

With regard to this collection, the Louvre possesses one of the most beautiful and important examples: the *Vergine d'Autun* by Jan van Eyck, also known as the *Virgin of Chancellor Rolin,* which is revolutionary for the open landscape behind the two main characters. Apart from the *Triptych of the Braque Family* by Rogier van der Weyden, attention should also be paid to the *Portrait of an Old Woman,* painted by Hans Memling around 1470-75, the *Banker and his Wife,* a typical painting of its kind by Quentin Metsys (1514), and *The Cripples* by Pieter Brueghel the Elder, an oil painting of small dimensions (18 by 21 cm) and of great emotional content. This group of five unfortunates shows a bit of everything: the comparison of the various social classes, the symbol of the sins of humanity and the depiction of the revolt of the 'gueux' of the Netherlands against the Spanish government of Philip II. The Flemish School of the 17th century revolved around Peter Paul Rubens. His 21 majestic paintings on the *Life of Maria de' Medici* should be noted as well as the delicate *Portrait of Hélène Fourment* and the dazzling *Kermesse,* where he admirably blends the colour experience of the Venetians with the Flemish tradition for open air dancing.

Pisanello, Portrait of a Princess of Este.

Jan van Eyck, The Madonna of Chancellor Rolin.

The 17th century is also similarly represented by the 'king's painter' Antoine van Dyck: his *Portrait of Charles I*, due to its absorbed psychological introspection, began and was the prototype in England for a deeply rooted tradition.

The Dutch School is also represented by great masters: Hieronymus Bosch with the *Ship of Fools*, Luke of Leyden, Frans Hals, who reveals frequent contacts with northern Caravaggism in the *Bohémienne*, and Johannes Vermeer, who transports us into the intimate surroundings of bourgeois houses: in the *Lace Vendor* (painted between 1664 and 1665), the perfect agreement between the lights, volumes, and colours transfigures the character from simplicity raising it to the highest levels of absolute values. And finally there is the glorious and numerous collection of works by Rembrandt, especially his portraits and self-portraits. We should particularly remember the *Self-Portrait* painted in 1660, *Bathsheba,* and *Supper at Emmaus*, in which the artist, at the height of his maturity, attains highly dramatic and mystical effects.

Although more modest, the **German collection** contains valuable works such as *Self-Portrait* by Dürer, *Venus* by Cranach, and the *Portrait of Erasmus* painted in 1523 by Hans Holbein the Younger, also the author of the *Portrait of Anne of Clèves* and the *Portrait of Nikolaus Kratzer.*

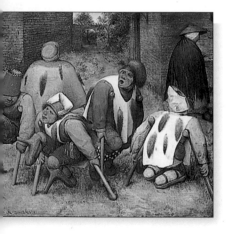

THE ENGLISH SCHOOL

England is represented at the Louvre by the great portrait-painters of the 17th century and first of all by Joshua Reynolds with his delicate and famous *Master Hare,* and Thomas Lawrence with the *Portraits of Julius Angerstein* and *His Wife.* The 19th century presents landscapes by Richard Parkes Bonington (*Mirror of Water at Versailles*), John Constable (*Bay of Weymouth*), and Joseph Turner (*Sea at Margate*).

Pieter Brueghel the Elder, The Cripples.

THE SPANISH SCHOOL

The Spanish School has many prestigious works and is distinguished above all by the great painting of the *Crucifixion* by El Greco, the *St Apollonia* and *Funeral of St Bonaventure* by Zurbarán, the *Young Beggar* and *Miracle of St James* by Murillo, *Portrait of the Infante Marguerite* and *Queen Mariana* by Diego Velasquez, and, finally, numerous portraits by Goya including *Woman with Fan* and above all the *Countess of Carpio,* one of his masterpieces painted around 1794, where the velvet black of the long skirt contrasts with the precious white lacework of the mantilla and the big pink ribbon, revealed by a few clever touches of light.

SCULPTURE

With regard to sculpture, it can be said that today the Louvre offers the most complete panorama of the history of sculpture from its origins up until the present day. We begin with the first Romanesque sculptures still closely linked to architectural functions, for instance decorated capitals, and then go on to the first examples of statues which complete the concept of sculpture as we know it today. Then there is the wealth of Gothic art, with sculptures from Chartres, Bourges, and Rheims (in particular the *funeral statue of Marie Bourbon*), and *the tomb of Philippe Pot* from the last quarter of the 15th century, created by Antoine le Moiturier for the Citeaux Abbey. The Renaissance period is documented by the works of two great sculptors: Jean Goujon and Germain Pilon. Of the former we should remember the reliefs of the *Fountain of the Innocents* and the *Deposition from the Cross with Four Evangelists*; by the latter, there is the delicate group of the *Three Graces* and the *statue of the Cardinal of Birague in Prayer*. The 17th and 18th centuries are represented by works of Pierre Puget, whose *Milo of Crotone* expresses all of the artist's dramatic genius; Simon Guillan with his *bronze statues of Anne of Austria, Louis XIII, and Louis XIV as a boy*, created for the Pont-au-Change monument; Antoine Coysevox with his *statues of the Seine* and the vigorous *Bust of Louis II of Bourbon*; Falconet, with a very delicate *Bather*; Jean-Antoine Houdon, whose art goes from the slender bronze depicting *Diana* to the terracottas with which he modelled the *Bust of Benjamin Franklin* and the *Bust of Louise Brongniart as a Girl*. Finally, we should not forget the famous *Love and Psyche*, sculpted by Canova in 1793, and the contrast offered by the joyful *The Dance* by Jean-Baptiste Carpeaux (1869).

Italian sculpture is represented by works of Nino Pisano, the Della Robbia family, Agostino di Duccio, Benedetto da Maiano *(Bust of Filippo Strozzi)*, Jacopo della Quercia *(Virgin and Child)*, and Desiderio da Settignano. Amongst the masterpieces are the *Rebellious Slave* and the *Dying Slave* by Michelangelo, sculpted between 1513 and 1515 for the tomb of Pope Julius II, Giambologna's *Mercury*, and the *Nymph of Fontainebleau* by Benvenuto Cellini.

A Slave by Michelangelo and a Cherub with Bow by Edme Bouchardon.

OBJETS D'ART

This section is of exceptional importance not only from an artistic but also a historical point of view. The most varied types of objects are gathered here, from furniture to tapestries, from jewellery to small bronzes, from miniatures to porcelains.

The Apollo Gallery, with the ceiling painted by Le Brun, hosts the Royal Treasury. Outstanding are the *Crown of St Louis*, the *Crown of Louis XV*, and that of *Napoleon I*; the *broche-reliquary* made for the Empress Eugenia in 1855; the *Hortensia Diamond* of 20 carats, the *Sancy Diamond* of 55 carats, and the splendid *Regent*, 136 carats, sent from Madras in England in 1702 by Thomas Pitt and bought for the French Crown in 1717 by the Duke of Orléans; some pieces from the *Treasury of St-Denis* and the *Treasury of the Order of St-Esprit*, founded by Henry II in 1578.

Along the rooms of the Colonnade, there is the reconstruction of the Council Room from the Palace of Vincennes; the ceiling with the facings and doors of the King's Ceremonial Chamber at the Louvre; the ivory *Harbeville Triptych* from the mid-10th century; the *reliquary arm of St Louis of Toulouse* in crystal and gilded silver; the tapestries of the *Hunt of Maximilian*, woven in Brussels to a design by Van Orley in 1535, and the tapestry of the *Martyrdom of St Mames* designed by Jean Cousin and woven by Pierre Blassé and Jacques Langlois. Then, in the Room of the Marshal of Effiat, there are the Gobelins tapestries depicting *Stories of Scipio* by Giulio Romano; furniture by the famous cabinet-maker André-Charles Boulle; the splendid, unique collection of snuff boxes, boxes for sweets, and other objects and clocks from the 17th and 18th centuries, decorated with chisel work, enamels, encrusted with precious stones and miniatures; the *writing desk of the King* by J. F. Oeben; the Chinese Room with a series of Chinese panels of painted paper from the end of the 18th century; Antoinette's dressing-case for travelling, made in Paris in 1787-88; the *Throne of Napoleon I*, made in 1804, and the *Cradle of the King of Rome*, made in 1811 to a design by Prud'hon; the Adolphe de Rothschild Collection with a basrelief by Agostino di Duccio depicting the *Virgin and Child with Angels*; the Camondo Collection, the Schlichting Collection, and the Thiers Collection with 18th century porcelains, Japanese lacquer work, and Chinese jade.

The Bather *by Étienne-Maurice Falconet and the celebrated* Barberini Ivory *(from Constantinople, late 5th - early 6th century).*

The Arch of Triumph at the Carrousel.

PLACE DU CARROUSEL – This garden occupies the site on which the Tuileries Palace stood before it burned down in 1871. The entrance portal is all that remains today of this magnificent palace. In 1964-1965 a sort of open-air museum was organised here, with many works of sculpture, among the most important being those by Aristide Maillol, including *Night* and the *Reclining Woman*.

CARROUSEL ARCH – Designed by Pierre-François Fontaine and Charles Percier, the arch was built between 1806 and 1808 and was intended to celebrate the victories of Napoleon Bonaparte in 1805. It imitates both the architectural design and the decoration of the Arch of Septimius Severus in Rome. Red and white marble columns frame the three archways and each side is filled with bas-reliefs which recall the Emperor's victories. On top of it were placed the four gilded horses which had been removed by order of Napoleon from the Venetian basilica of San Marco, to which they were returned in 1815. The originals were then replaced by copies, and a chariot and the *statue of Peace* were added later.

3rd Itinerary

3rd Itinerary

From Palais-Royal
to the Élysée Palace

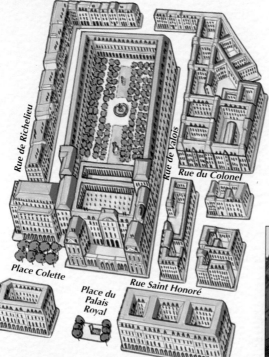

Rue de Richelieu

Rue de Valois

Rue du Colonel

Place Colette

Rue Saint Honoré

Place du
Palais
Royal

The façade of the church of St-Germain-l'Auxerrois.

ST-GERMAIN-L'AUXERROIS

Also called the 'Grande Paroisse' (Great Parish Church) because it was the royal chapel of the Louvre in the 14th century, the present Church of St-Germain stands on the site of a previous sanctuary dating from the Merovingian era. Its construction took from the 12th to the 16th century. On the façade is a deep porch in Gothic style (1435-1439), with five arches, each one different from the others, and statues adorning the pillars which divide them. Above the porch is the rose window, surmounted by a cusp, and alongside it the bell tower (11th century).

Interior. The church's interior is impressive, including nave and double aisles divided by pillars, transept, and chancel. It contains a wealth of art works. Worth noting is the **royal pew,** carved from wood by F. Mercier in 1682. Also in polychrome wood is the statue of *St Germanus,* while that of *St Vincent* is of stone; both are from the 15th century. *A Flemish altarpiece* in carved wood depicts *Scenes from the Life of Christ.* The stained-glass windows in the transept date to the 15th century.

RUE DE RIVOLI – This street runs parallel to the Seine between Place de la Concorde and Place de la Bastille. It owes its name to the victory which Napoleon won against Austria at Rivoli in 1797.
One side of the street is lined with elegant porticos where today are located grand hotels, like the Meurice at no. 228, and celebrated shops like the city's first English bookseller's establishment, Galignani, inaugurated in 1800.

PLACE DES PYRAMIDES – This small square lies in front of the Pavillon de Marsan; in the centre is the *equestrian statue of Joan of Arc* (Frémiet, 1874), to which on 12 May every year many people make a pilgrimage.

UNION CENTRALE DES ARTS DÉCORATIFS – At no. 107 Rue de Rivoli we find the UCAD (Union Centrale des Arts Décoratifs), home to three important collections: the **Musée des Arts Décoratifs**, the **Musée de la Mode et du Textile**, and the recently-founded **Musée de la Publicité**.

The first of the three possesses more than 140,000 items in collections that range from the Middle Ages to the present; the most important pieces are sculpted and painted altarpieces, tapestries, and sculptures. The Art Nouveau and Art Déco collections are also worth a visit, as is the collection of Islamic art.

The Musée de la Mode et du Textile collection of more than 125,000 items between clothes and accessories has recently been enriched by substantial donations from private collectors, fashion houses, and designers. Every year, the Museum stages a new theme exhibit in an original setting.

Finally, the Musée de la Publicité: housed in a structure designed by Jean Nouvel, it is the first museum of its kind in the world. Its collections cover all branches of advertising: 50,000 posters from the mid-18th century through World War II (with works by Toulouse-Lautrec, Mucha, Binhard, Beardsley, Utrillo, Klimt, and others) and another 50,000 from 1950 to the present, examples of cinema, television, and radio advertising from 1930 to the present, thousands of advertisements from newspapers and magazines (French and otherwise), hundreds of radio jingles, and finally a multimedia system located in the interactive space known as the 'Square' that is the natural extension of the Museum.

The equestrian statue of Joan of Arc in Place des Pyramides.

The double colonnade of the Court of Honour in the Palais-Royal.
The steel balls of the fountain are by Pol Bury.

PALAIS-ROYAL

Built by Lemercier between 1624 and 1645, this palace was originally the private residence of Cardinal Richelieu, who on his death in 1642 left it to Louis XIII. Today it is the seat of the Council of State, the Constitutional Court, and the Ministry of Culture. It has a façade with columns erected in 1774 and a small courtyard from which one passes through a double colonnade into a splendid and famous garden. This garden was planned by Victor Louis in 1781 and extends for some 225 metres. Three wings of robust pillars surround it, and the portico thus formed is occupied today by extremely interesting shops selling old objects and rare books. During the Revolution, it became the meeting-place of patriots: in fact here the anti-monarchical nobles met, and among this group was the Duke of Orléans, who was later to rename himself Philippe-Égalité.

PLACE DES VICTOIRES – This square, circular in form, came into being in 1685 as a surrounding for the allegorical statue of Louis XIV, commissioned from Desjardins by the Duke de la Feuillade. The statue was destroyed during the Revolution and in 1822 replaced by another made by Bosio. The square was created under the direction of Jules Hardouin-Mansart, and important figures came to live here: the Duke de la Feuillade himself occupied nos. 2 and 4, while the financier Crozat lived at no. 3.

NOTRE-DAME-DES-VICTOIRES – The church belonged to a monastery of the Barefooted Augustinians. The foundation stone was laid by Louis XIII in 1629, but it was not completed until 1740. Important pilgrimages to the Virgin have been held here since 1836, and in the church there are more than 30,000 votive offerings. The **interior** is without aisles, but has linking chapels along the sides. In the second chapel on the left is the

The equestrian statue of Louis XIV in Place des Victoires.

cenotaph of the Florentine composer Lulli, who died in 1687. In the chancel are 17th-century wood carvings and seven canvases by Van Loo, depicting *Scenes from the Life of St Augustine* and *Louis XIII Dedicating the Church to the Virgin.*

NATIONAL LIBRARY

The main entrance is at no. 58 Rue de Richelieu (in front of the Square Louvois, with its fine fountain made by Visconti in 1844).
From the entrance one passes directly into the monumental courtyard, a work by Robert de Cotte (18th century). From here, on the right, one reaches the vestibule, where the finest books held by the library under copyright law are displayed. The vestibule leads in turn to the library's various departments. At the end is the Galerie Mansart, where important exhibitions are often held; opposite is the State Room, with the original plaster bust of Voltaire by Houdon. The monumental staircase leads up to the first floor, with the splendid Galerie Mazarine designed by Mansart and with paintings by G. F. Romanelli.

Since 1996, almost all of the books formerly kept here have been moved to the brand-new Bibliothéque Nationale de France in the Tolbiac quarter. Here, instead, there have remained the most precious and rarest manuscripts and publications: two exemplars of the Gutenberg *Bible*, original manuscripts by Victor Hugo and Marcel Proust, valuable miniatures such as Charlemagne's *Evangelary*, Charles the Bald's *Bible*, Saint Louis'

Louis XIV (1643 - 1715), the *Roi Soleil*

At the death of Cardinal Mazarin, Louis XIV declared that he intended to reign alone and that he himself would have acted as Prime Minister. Snubbing Paris, he began construction, at Versailles, of the sumptuous palace in which the rulers of France lived until 1789. He personally supervised the works, imposing his tastes and his ideas over those of Le Vau as regarded the layout of the palace, Le Brun the interiors, and Le Nôtre the gardens.
It is said that on his deathbed, Louis XIV confessed to having loved two things too much - war, and buildings.

Psalter, and the *Livre d'Heures de Rohan*. The National Library is also home to the Cabinet of Medals and Antiquities, with coins and medals of all historical eras, and the Treasures of St-Denis and of the Sainte-Chapelle.

PLACE DU THÉÂTRE FRANÇAIS – This colourful square lies at the end of the Avenue de l'Opéra. In it is France's most important prose theatre, the **Comédie-Française,** founded in 1680 by the merging of Molière's company of actors with those of the Hôtel de Bourgogne. In 1812, a special statute was created for the company by Napoleon (the 'Décret de Moscou').

The repertoire of the Comédie ranges from the French classics (Molière above all, followed by Racine, Corneille, etc.) to the modern French writers (Claudel and Anouihl), besides foreigners (Pirandello). The building was erected by Victor Louis in 1786-1790, and its façade was added by Chabrol in 1850. In the vestibule and in the foyer can be seen the *statues* of the great dramatic writers: *Voltaire* and *Molière* (by Houdon), *Victor Hugo* (by Dalou), *Dumas* (by Carpeaux), and others. Also to be seen is the chair in which Molière was sitting on stage, while acting in his *Imaginary Invalid*, when hit by a fatal illness on 17 February 1673.

RUE ST-HONORÉ – This is one of the oldest streets in Paris: in fact it existed as far back as the 12th century. Furthermore, it is a street filled with memories of the Revolution: the club of the Feuillants was here, and not far away the club of the Jacobins, headed by Robespierre. The street was also on the route along which the carts passed carrying those condemned to death from the Conciergerie prison to the guillotine in Place de la Concorde.

CHURCH OF ST-ROCH – In Rue St-Honoré, the Church of St-Roch is extremely interesting because of the works of art it contains. It was begun under Louis XIV in 1653 and finished a century later; in 1736 the façade was erected by Robert de Cotte. The **interior**, in a sumptuous Baroque style, has three aisles with side chapels, transept, chancel, and ambulatory with radial chapels; behind the chancel is a vast round chapel, the **Lady Chapel,** with a ring-shaped nave and semicircular apse (built by Hardouin-Mansart); behind the Lady Chapel is a rectangular chapel called the **Calvary Chapel.**
The church's chapels contain the remains of Corneille, Diderot, and Le Nôtre.

A fountain in Place André Malraux.

The statue of Molière in Place du Théâtre Français.

The façade of the church of St-Roch.

Place Vendôme by night and as it
appeared in the early 20th century.

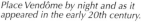

PLACE VENDÔME

A vast architectural complex dating from the time of
Louis XIV, its name derives from the fact that the residence of the Duke of Vendôme was here. It was created
between 1687 and 1720 as a setting for the equestrian statue by Girardon dedicated to Louis XIV and destroyed during the Revolution. The square, octagonal in form, simple
and austere, is surrounded by buildings which have large
arcades on the ground floor and skilfully distributed pediments higher up, crowned on the roofs by the dormer windows typical of Paris. Today at no. 15 is the famous Hôtel
Ritz and at no. 12 the house where Chopin died in 1849.
In the centre of the square is the **column** erected by
Gondouin and Lepère between 1806 and 1810 in honour
of Napoleon I. Inspired by the Column of Trajan in Rome,
it is 43.5 metres high with, around its shaft, a spiralling
series of bronze bas-reliefs cast from the 1,200 cannon cap-
tured at Austerlitz. On the top of the column, Chaudet
erected a statue of the Emperor dressed as Caesar, but it
was destroyed in 1814 and replaced with a statue of Henri
IV. This was replaced in 1863, this time by a statue of the
Little Corporal in military dress, which eight years later, at
the time of the Commune, was once more pulled down. It
was finally replaced three years later by a copy of the
original statue by Chaudet.

59

From Place Vendôme, we walk along **Rue de la Paix,** which was previously called Rue Napoléon. Today it is one of the most splendid streets in the city, lined by famous and expensive shops: at no. 13 is the jeweller Cartier. At the end of the street on the right we reach the **Avenue de l'Opéra,** which was opened at the time of the Second Empire.

Place Vendôme, the Drawing-room of Paris

Since the time of the Second Empire, Place Vendôme has been a synonym of luxury, vanity, and - why not? - magic.

The come-hither spell cast by the shop windows of its world-famous jewellers is irresistible - a walk around the square has become a 'must' to the point of having taken on the connotations of an almost formal rite. The doors of the various *maisons* open on elegant interiors where velvets and *boiseries* create subdued settings for a unique kind of shopping.

As early as 1700, Chaumet was creating jewels for the European courts: theirs is the parure set in rubies and diamonds that the founder Marie-Étienne Nitot fashioned for the marriage of Napoleon I and Marie Louise of Austria; theirs is the tiara, made using the crown jewels, given by the French emperor to Pope Pius VII. The collection of royal diadems is displayed in the singular museum in the Hôtel St James, where the boutique is also located.

Since 1946, Place Vendôme also hosts the show-windows of Mauboussin, among whose most famous pieces is the bracelet with cabochon emerald given by Charles Chaplin to Paulette Goddard (when she was excluded from the cast of *Gone with the Wind*).

Then there are the show windows of Mikimoto, with their extremely rare black pearls, and those of the Italians Bulgari and Buccellati. Separated in time by about ten years the one from the other (1893 and 1906, respectively) were the openings, on the square, of the *maisons* of Boucheron and of Van Cleef & Arpels, who brought extraordinary innovations to the field of jewellery

Other stopping-places include the elegant windows of the Italian Repossi and the Russian Alexandre Reza, with his pronounced preference for the big stones, before turning off into the Rue de la Paix, the realm of Cartier, the world's best-known jeweller, he who the English king Edward VII defined as 'the jeweller of kings, the king of jewellers'.

But how can we abandon this square without having spared at least a glance for the Hôtel Ritz, the hundred-year's chronicle of which is linked to so many great events in the history of Paris?

The Hôtel Ritz was created in 1898 by the Swiss César Ritz, whose stated intent was to assure to the rich clientele of his establishment 'all the refinement that a prince could desire in his own home'. And thus he transformed the palace of the Duke of Lauzun at no. 15 Place Vendôme into that which was to become one of the world's premier hotels. Or, if nothing else, the most famous.

Guests at the Ritz have included writers and politicians, movie stars and crowned heads, intellectuals and Arab princes, industrial magnates and financial tycoons.

Marcel Proust wrote a part of his *Remembrance of Things Past* here; for the Dukes of Windsor was reserved a 'fairy-tale' suite; Coco Chanel, who lived in an apartment here for 35 years, may have taken her inspiration for the face of her famous *Première* watch from the magical form of the square below her windows.

The lavish façade of the Opéra, by night.

OPÉRA

The Opéra is the largest theatre for lyric opera in the world (it covers an area of 11,000 square metres and can accommodate an audience of 2,000 and 450 performers on the stage). Designed by Garnier and built between 1862 and 1875, it is the most typical monument of the era of Napoleon III.

An ample stairway leads up to the first of the two orders into which the façade is divided, with its large arcades and robust pillars, in front of which are numerous marble groups. The finest is the one in front of the second pillar on the right: *La Danse* by Jean-Baptiste Carpeaux. The second order consists of tall double columns framing large windows; above is an attic, with exuberant decoration, on which the flattened cupola rests. The **interior** is just as highly adorned: its great staircase is enriched by marbles, the vault is decorated with paintings by Isidore Pils, and the hall has a large fresco by Marc Chagall (1966).

The Opéra stands at the beginning of the **Boulevard des Capucines,** so called because near here stood a convent of Capuchin nuns. At no. 28 is the **Olympia,** the famous music-hall; at no. 14 an epigraph recalls that here, on 28 December 1895, the Lumière brothers projected a film for the first time in public. In 1842, on the footpath in front of what is now the Ministry for Foreign Affairs, Stendhal collapsed after an apoplectic stroke.

The classical façade of La Madeleine.

LA MADELEINE

Designed along the lines of the Maison Carrée at Nîmes, the Madeleine was built by order of Napoleon in honour of the Grand Army. He had a previous building, which had never been completed, demolished and in 1806 commissioned the architect Vignon to begin building. In 1814 it became a church and was dedicated to St Mary Magdalen. It has the form and structure of a classical Greek temple: a wide base with a stairway, and a colonnade of 52 Corinthian columns, each 20 metres high. The pediment has a huge frieze sculpted by Lemaire in 1834, depicting the *Last Judgment*.

Interior. The building is without aisles. In the vestibule are two groups of sculpture by Pradier and Rudel. Above the high alter is a work by Marochetti (*Assumption of St Mary Magdalen*).

Pierre-Antoine Demachy, the interior of La Madeleine as planned by Constant d'Ivry.

In front of the Madeleine, the **Rue Royale** stretches out in a fine perspective, closed at the other end by the symmetrical mass of the Palais Bourbon. The Rue Royale, opened in 1732, is short but full of luxury: at no. 3 is the celebrated Maxim's restaurant, with its Art Nouveau interiors; at no. 11 the Crystal of Lalique; at no. 12 the silver of Christofle; at no. 16, for the sweet-toothed, the famous Ladurée pastry-shop.

About halfway along Rue Royale is another important street, **Rue du Faubourg St-Honoré,** of which the number 13 was removed by order of the superstitious Empress Eugénie. This street has become almost synonymous with elegance and fashion, since it contains some of the most famous shops for perfumes, jewellery, and dresses in the world. Among their names are St-Laurent, Hermès, Cardin, Lancôme, Helena Rubinstein, Carita, and Lanvin.

Rue Royale at the turn of the last century.

One side of the Élysée Palace faces on Rue du Faubourg St-Honoré.

ÉLYSÉE PALACE

This is the residence of the President of the French Republic. It was built in 1718 by Mollet for the son-in-law of the financier Crozat, the Count d'Evreux. After becoming public property during the Revolution, it was inhabited by Caroline Bonaparte and later by the Empress Josephine. Here, on 22 June 1815, Napoleon signed his act of abdication. Since 1873, the Élysée has been the official residence of the various presidents who have headed the French Republic.

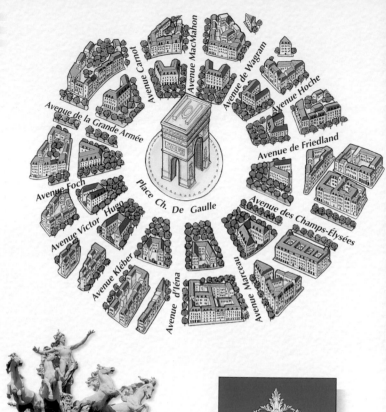

Avenue Carnot
Avenue MacMahon
Avenue de Wagram
Avenue Hoche
Avenue de la Grande Armée
Avenue de Friedland
Avenue Foch
Place Ch. De Gaulle
Avenue des Champs-Élysées
Avenue Victor Hugo
Avenue Kléber
Avenue d'Iéna
Avenue Marceau

4th Itinerary
Place de la Concorde and the Champs-Élysées

PLACE DE LA CONCORDE

Laid out by Jacques-Ange Gabriel between 1757 and 1779, the square was originally dedicated to Louis XV, of whom there was an equestrian statue in the centre by Pigalle and Bouchardon, pulled down during the Revolution. In its place the guillotine was erected, and among those who died here were King Louis XVI, his queen Marie-Antoinette, Danton, Madame Roland, Robespierre, and St Just. The square assumed its present appearance between 1836 and 1840, when it was replanned by the architect Hittorf. In the centre stands the **Egyptian obelisk** from the temple of Luxor, given in 1831 by Mohammed Alì to

From the plays of water of the fountain in Place de la Concorde emerge the forms of the obelisk and the two majestic palaces that close off the square.

The square seen from the gates leading in to the Tuileries.

Louis-Philippe and erected in 1836. It is 23 metres high and is adorned with hieroglyphics which illustrate the deeds of the pharaoh Rameses II. At the corners of the square are the eight statues which symbolise the main cities of France. On the northern side, the two colonnaded buildings (designed by Gabriel) today contain the **Ministry of the Navy** and the **Hôtel Crillon**.

TUILERIES GARDENS – The gardens extend for about one kilometre between Place de la Concorde and Place du Carrousel. Entrance is through an imposing gate with pillars bearing the **equestrian statues of Mercury** (on the right) and **Fame** (on the left), both by Coysevox.
Two flights of steps lead up to the terraces of the Orangerie (to the right) and of the Jeune de Paume (to the left), which until recently housed the Impressionist collections now on display at the Musée d'Orsay on the left bank of the Seine. Nowadays temporary exhibitions are held at the Jeu de Paume.

Evocative plays of light on the obelisk in Place de la Concorde.

A side avenue in the Tuileries leading toward the Carrousel Garden.

A view of the
Musée d'Orsay
from the Seine,
and the old Gare
d'Orsay.

A statue at the
entrance to the
Musée d'Orsay.

© Musée d'Orsay Fond. Urphot

MUSÉE D'ORSAY

What the press defined as 'the most beautiful museum in Europe' is to be found on the left bank of the Seine, where the State Audit Court, destroyed during the Commune, originally stood in 1870. In 1898, the Paris-Orléans railway company assigned the building of the new station to Victor Laloux. The work was carried out in two years so that the Gare d'Orsay was ready for the universal exhibition held in 1900. Laloux designed a grandiose nave, 135 metres by 40 metres, the metal structure of which was skilfully covered on the outside by light-coloured stucco work. The interior not only housed the sixteen platforms but also restaurants and an elegant hotel with at least 400 rooms. Abandoned in 1939, the Gare d'Orsay went on a slow decline under the spectre of demolition: Orson Welles's cultural revival with the filming of *The Trial* or the establishment of Jean-Louis Barrault's company there were of no avail. In 1973, the French President at the time, Georges Pompidou, declared it a national monument and saw to it that a museum displaying the half century of art that goes from Napoleon III's Second Empire to the beginnings of Cubism was established there. It proved to be a perfect link between the Louvre, a temple of ancient art, and the Centre Georges Pompidou, a temple of modern art. The tender for contract for its restructuring commenced in 1978 and was won by the ACT group; the Italian architect Ms Gae Aulenti was entrusted with the interior decorating. Nowadays more than 4,000 works, including paintings, sculptures, drawings, and furniture, are exhibited in over 45,000 square metres.

The unique interior of the museum.

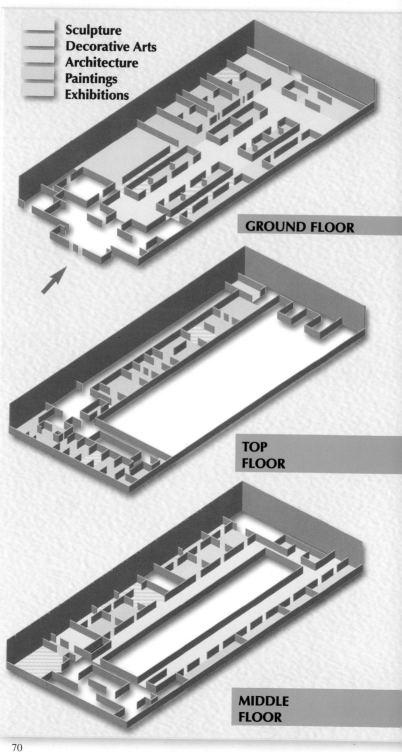

Sculpture
Decorative Arts
Architecture
Paintings
Exhibitions

GROUND FLOOR

TOP FLOOR

MIDDLE FLOOR

70

Toulouse-Lautrec: **La Toilette**

P. Cézanne: **Les Joueurs de carte**

A. Charpentier: **Dining-room**

V. Van Gogh: **Self-portrait**

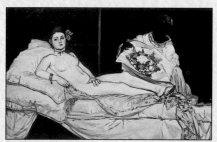

E. Manet: **Olympia**

E. Manet: **Le Déjeuner sur l'herbe**

E. Gallé: **Glass cupboard of the dragonflies**

Vincent Van Gogh, Vincent's Room in Arles.

Paul Cézanne, Apples and Oranges.

The **ground floor** features paintings, sculptures and decorative arts from 1850 to 1870, with works by Ingres, Delacroix, Manet, Puvis de Chavannes, and Gustave Moreau. Impressionist paintings (Monet, Renoir, Pissarro, Degas, and Manet), the Personnaz, Gachet, and Guillaumin Collections, and Post-Impressionist paintings, with masterpieces by Seurat, Signac, Toulouse-Lautrec, Gauguin, Van Gogh, and the Nabis group (Bonnard, Vuillard, and Vallotton), are displayed on the **top floor.** Lastly, the **middle floor** features art from 1870 to 1914, with the official art of the Third Republic, Symbolism, academic painting, and the decorative arts of the Art Nouveau period, with Guimard, Émile Gallé, and the School of Nancy.

Claude Monet, The Cathedral of Rouen.

Paul Gauguin, Arearea (Joyfulness).

Jean-Auguste Ingres, The Source.

Paul Gauguin, sculpted wooden mask.

Auguste Renoir, Dance at the
Moulin de la Galette.

Georges Stein, The Arch of Triumph.

Facing page, the side of the arch facing the Champs-Élysées, with the bas-relief of the Marseillaise on the right.

CHAMPS-ÉLYSÉES

This was originally a vast swampy area; after its reclamation, in 1667 Le Nôtre designed the wide avenue which was first called the Grand-Cours (its present name dates from 1709): it extends from the Tuileries to Place de l'Étoile, now called Place de Gaulle. At the beginning of the avenue are the celebrated **Horses of Marly** by Guillaume Coustou. From here to the Rond-Point of the Champs-Élysées, the avenue is flanked by a vast park. As we walk along it, on the right is the **Théâtre des Ambassadeurs - Espace Pierre Cardin** and on the left the **Ledoyen restaurant** from the time of Louis XVI. In **Place Clemenceau** is the bronze *statue* of this famous politician who led France to victory in 1918. At this point the panoramic **Avenue Churchill** begins, with the Alexandre III Bridge and the Invalides in the background. On each side of the Avenue Churchill are the Grand Palais and the Petit Palais, two imposing buildings with large colonnades, friezes, and sculptural groups, erected for the World Fair held in Paris in 1900.

A nocturnal view of the Champs-Élysées and the Arch of Triumph

ROND-POINT of the Champs-Élysées – This important intersection is at the end of the park zone of the Champs-Élysées; the square, about 140 metres wide, was designed by Le Nôtre. On the right is the headquarters of the newspaper *Le Figaro*, on the left that of *Jours de France*. This is the beginning of the broad street (its two footpaths are each 22 metres wide and the roadway 27) along either side of which are the offices of airlines, banks, and automobile showrooms.

PLACE DE GAULLE – Formerly Place de l'Étoile, this square is at the end of the Champs-Élysées. It is a vast circular area 120 metres in diameter, from which a total of twelve important streets radiate out: Avenue des Champs-Élysées, Avenue de Friedland, Avenue Hoche, Avenue de Wagram, Avenue MacMahon, Avenue Carnot, Avenue de la Grande Armée, Avenue Foch, Avenue Victor Hugo, Avenue Kléber, Avenue d'Iéna, and Avenue Marceau.

ARCH OF TRIUMPH

The massive arch stands in majestic isolation in the centre of the square. Ordered by Napoleon as a memorial to the Grand Army, it was begun by Chalgrin in 1806. Completed in 1836, it has a single archway and actually exceeds in size the Arch of Constantine in Rome: it is 50 metres high and 45 wide. On the faces of the arch are bas-reliefs, the best known and finest piece being that on the right, on the part of the arch facing the Champs-Élysées, depicting the departure of the volunteers in 1792 and known as the **Marseillaise** (F. Rude). The bas-reliefs higher up celebrate the victories of Napoleon, while the shields sculpted on the attic bear the names of the great battles. The Tomb of the Unknown Soldier was placed under the arch in 1920.

GRAND PALAIS – Built by Daglane and Louvet, with a façade 240 metres long with 20-metre Ionic columns. Today art shows, including important exhibitions of painting, are held here.
Part of it is occupied by the **Palais de la Découverte,** or Palace of Discovery, where the most recent conquests of science and the steps in man's progress are celebrated.

View of the Grand Palais.

PETIT PALAIS – Home to the Musée du Petit Palais, a large collection of ancient and modern art. It includes the paintings by French artists of the 19th and 20th centuries (from Géricault to Delacroix, from Ingres to Courbet, from Redon to Bonnard), which are part of the **Municipal Collections.** The **Tuck** and **Dutuit Collections,** on the other hand, include not only various objects of Greek, Roman, Etruscan, and Egyptian antiquity (among them enamel work and pottery) but also drawings and paintings from various eras and various countries (including works by Dürer, Cranach, Van de Velde, Watteau, Pollaiolo, Guardi).

PONT ALEXANDRE III – This is at the end of the Avenue Winston Churchill. It consists of a single metal span, 107 metres long and 40 wide, linking the Esplanade des Invalides and the Champs-Élysées.
It was built between 1896 and 1900 to celebrate the alliance between Russia and France, and is named after Czar Alexander III, whose son, Nicholas II, performed its inauguration. On the two piers on the right bank are the statues representing medieval France and modern France, while those on the left bank represent Renaissance France and the France of Louis XIV. On the bridge's entrance piers are allegories of the rivers Seine and Neva, symbolising France and Russia. The whole bridge has exuberant decorations with cherubs, allegorical marine deities, garlands of flowers, and lamps supported by cherubs.

The lovely façade of the Petit Palais.

Pont Alexandre III and details
of the rich sculptural
decoration.

5th Itinerary

We now move on to the Chaillot quarter, which we reach via the Avenue d'Iéna as far as the square of the same name. In the centre is an *equestrian statue of George Washington*, a gift from the women of America. The modern building with its rotunda on the corner of the square is now the headquarters of the Economic and Social Council (Perret, 1938).

MUSÉE GUIMET (National Museum of Asiatic Art) – Entrance at no. 6. Founded by the art collector Émile Guimet from Lyons, it gives a complete panorama of the art of the East and Far East. It includes works of art from India (among them the *Cosmic Dance of Siva*), Cambodia (collection of Khmer art), Nepal, Tibet (*Dancing Dakini* in gilt bronze), Afghanistan, Pakistan, China, and Japan.

PALAIS GALLIERA – This is nearby, its entrance at no. 10 Avenue Pierre Ier-de-Serbie. The building, in Renaissance style, was erected for the Duchess of Galliera in 1889 to house her art collections. These were eventually left to the city of Genoa, while the building was left to Paris. The museum now hosts the **Musée de la Mode et du Costume**.

PALAIS DE TOKYO – This is situated at no. 13 Avenue du Président Wilson and was built for the Exhibition of 1937. It consists of two separate sections, linked by a portico above. Between the two wings is a basin with bas-reliefs and statues around it. Three large bronze statues by Bourdelle represent *France*, *Strength*, and *Victory*. The building is home to the Musée d'Art Moderne de la Ville de Paris (Museum of Modern Art of the City of Paris) and the Centre Nationale de la Photografie.

MUSÉE D'ART MODERNE DE LA VILLE DE PARIS (Museum of Modern Art of the City of Paris) – This museum's collections of paintings serve to recall the importance which the Parisian school had in the development of painting in the 20th century.

On this page, some of the stone and bronze sculptures in Palais de Chaillot.

It contains paintings by Modigliani, Rouault, Utrillo, Picasso, Dufy, Vlaminck, Derain, and others, and sculpture by Zadkin, Maillol, and others. The largest picture in the world is also exhibited here: the *Fée Electricité*, by Dufy, with an area of nearly 600 square meters.

From here we move on to **Place du Trocadéro,** the name of which derives from a Spanish fortress which the French conquered in 1823. In the centre is the equestrian *statue of Marshal Foch* (R. Wlérick and R. Martin, 1951). At the corner of Avenue Georges-Mandel is the wall of the **Passy Cemetery.** In it are buried a number of great men: the painters *Manet* and *Berthe Morisot*, the writers *Giraudoux* and *Tristan Bernard*, and the composers *Debussy* and *Fauré. Las Cases*, the companion of Napoleon during his exile on St Helena, is also buried here.

Nearby is the Passy quarter, known in the past for its iron-rich waters. At no. 8 Rue Franklin is the **Clemenceau Museum,** occupying the apartment of the great statesman (known as the 'Tiger'), which has been kept exactly as it was on the day of his death in 1929 and which contains documents and souvenirs of his long career as a journalist and politician.

At no. 47 Rue Raynouard is the house inhabited by Balzac from 1840 to 1847, now a museum containing various objects which belonged to the great writer. Finally, at no. 116 of Avenue Président Kennedy, is the **Maison de Radio-France,** headquarters of French Radio and Television, built between 1959 and 1964 by H. Bernard with a 70-metre tower, 1000 offices, 62 studios, and five auditoriums.

PALAIS DE CHAILLOT – Along with the gardens of the Trocadéro, the Champs-Élysées, and the Eiffel Tower, the Palais de Chaillot constitutes a fine example of early 20th-century architecture. It was built for the Exhibition held in Paris in 1937. Its architects were Boileau, Azéma, and Carlu, who planned the present building on the site of previous structure, the Trocadéro. The Chaillot Palace consists of two enormous pavilions which stretch out in two wings, united by a central terrace with statues of gilt bronze. The two pavilions, on the front of which are engraved verses by the poet Valéry, today contain the **Musée de la Marine**, the **Musée de l'Homme**, and the **Musée des Monuments Français**.

MUSÉE DE LA MARINE – This is one of the richest naval museums in the world. It contains models of ships, original objects, souvenirs, and works of art linked to the sea.

Above, a gilded bronze sculpture decorating a fountain at Chaillot.

The Trocadéro seen from the Eiffel Tower, in a view from the early 1900s.

The Palais de Chaillot with its large pool and gardens.

Among these are the model of Columbus' ship the *Santa Maria*, and the ship *La Belle Poule*, which brought the ashes of Napoleon back to France from St Helena.

MUSÉE DE L'HOMME – The Museum of Man contains important collections of anthropology and ethnology, illustrating the various human races and their ways of life. In the gallery of palaeontology, there are some very famous prehistoric discoveries: the *Venus of Lespugue*, made from mammoth's ivory, a cast of the *Hottentot Venus*, and the *Hoggar frescoes*.

MUSÉE DES MONUMENTS FRANÇAIS – Born in 1880 from an idea of Viollet-le-Duc, the Museum of French Monuments offers a vast artistic panorama from the Carolingian period on. The works are grouped according to regions, schools, and periods, so that the visitor can study the evolution, characteristics, and influence of each style.

Also in the complex of the Palais de Chaillot is the **Théâtre de Chaillot,** situated below the terrace, with a capacity of 3000 persons. In 1948 and in 1951-1952 it was used for the third and sixth sessions of the General Assembly of the United Nations.

In a grotto in the garden is the **Aquarium,** in which the life of most of the freshwater fishes from all over France can be observed. The gardens slope gently down to the Seine, which the **Pont d'Iéna** (1813) crosses here. Adorned with four equestrian groups at the ends, the bridge links Place de Varsovie to the other bank, dominated by the Eiffel Tower.

On this and the following two pages, views of the Eiffel Tower. The two period photographs on page 84 were taken while the tower was being built.

EIFFEL TOWER

The Eiffel Tower, which has become the symbol of Paris, was erected for the World Fair in 1889. A masterpiece designed by the engineer Gustave Eiffel, it is altogether 320 metres high, an extremely light, interlaced structure made of 15,000 pieces of metal welded together. Its weight of 7000 tons rests on four huge piers with cement bases. It has three floors: the first at 57 metres, the second at 115, and the third at 274. Bars and restaurants on the first two allow the tourist to pause and enjoy the astonishing view.

Gustave Eiffel photographed with his aides.

The Champ-de-Mars seen from the Eiffel Tower.

CHAMP-DE-MARS – This carpet of green stretching beneath the Eiffel Tower was originally a military parade ground, but was later transformed into a garden. During the Ancien Régime and the Revolution, many festivals were held here, including the famous Festival of the Supreme Being introduced by Robespierre and celebrated on 8 June 1794. In modern times, the area has been the site of numerous World Fairs. Today the garden, the design of which was supervised by Formigé between 1908 and 1928, is divided by wide paths and embellished by small lakes, watercourses, and flower beds.

MILITARY ACADEMY – The École Militaire, the French Military Academy, stands at the end of the panoramic Champ-de-Mars. Built on the initiative of the financier Pâris-Duverney and of Madame Pompadour, who wanted young men of the poorer

The centre façade of the École Militaire.

classes to be able to take up military careers, it was built between 1751 and 1773 by the architect Jacques-Ange Gabriel. The façade has two orders of windows and in the centre is a pavilion with columns which support the pediment; it is decorated with statues and covered by a cupola. The graceful **Courtyard of Honour** has a portico of twin Doric columns and the façade is formed by three pavilions linked by two rows of columns. Napoleon Bonaparte entered the academy in 1784 and left the following year with the rank of second lieutenant in the artillery.

The grandiose complex that is Les Invalides.

UNESCO BUILDING – Standing behind the Military Academy, it was constructed in 1955-1958 by three great modern architects: the American Breuer, the Italian Nervi, and the Frenchman Zehrfuss. They planned it as a Y-shaped building with large windows and a curving front. Great artists collaborated in the decoration and embellishment of the vast complex, among whom Henry Moore, Calder, Mirò, Jean Arp, Picasso, and Le Corbusier.

LES INVALIDES

Stretching between Place Vauban and the Esplanade des Invalides, this vast complex of buildings includes the Hôtel des Invalides, the Dôme, and the Church of St-Louis.
The whole construction, which Louis XIV ordered built and the commission for which was given to Libéral Bruant in 1671, was designed as a refuge for old and invalid soldiers, who were then

often forced to beg for a living. The vast square of the **Esplanade** (1704-1720) is 487 metres long and 250 wide, creating perfect surroundings for the **Hôtel.** In the garden in front of the *hôtel* bronze cannon of the 17th and 18th century are lined up, eighteen pieces belonging to the 'triumphal battery' which was fired only on important occasions. The façade, 196 metres long, has four orders of windows and a majestic portal in the centre, surmounted by a relief representing *Louis XIV* with *Prudence* and *Justice* at his sides.

In the courtyard, the four sides consist of two levels of arcades, and the pavilion at the end becomes the façade of the Church of St-Louis. In the centre is the *statue* by Seurre depicting *Napoleon* (previously on top of the Vendôme Column). The **Church of St-Louis-des-Invalides,** designed by Hardouin-Mansart, has three aisles. Many flags hang from its walls. In the crypt, Rouget de Lisle, author of the Marseillaise, is buried together with the Marshals of France and Governors of Les Invalides.

The Hôtel des Invalides today hosts important museums: the **Musée de l'Armée,** the **Musée d'Histoire Contemporaine,** and the **Musée des Plans-Reliefs**. The first, the Museum

Les Invalides from Pont Alexandre III and, below, the façade of the Hôtel, dominated by the gilded mass of the Dôme.

of the Army, is the richest military-oriented collection in the world, with not only weapons and armour from 1300 through the present but also mementos and historical relics of great importance and value.

DÔME DES INVALIDES

The fine gate at the entrance.

The Dôme, with its entrance in Place Vauban, is the real masterpiece of Hardouin-Mansart, who built it between 1679 and 1706. It has a square plan and two orders. The façade above all is a work of elegance and symmetry: above the two orders of columns surmounted by a pediment is the solid mass of the drum with its twin columns. Soaring above this, after a sober series of corbels, is the slim cupola, decorated with garlands and floral motifs. Covered with gilt leaves, the cupola terminates in a small lantern with spire, 107 metres above ground level.

Interior. In the form of a Greek cross, it is as simple as the exterior. The *Four Evangelists* painted in the pendentives of the cupola are by Charles de la Fosse, who also painted the large figure of *St Louis Presenting Christ with his Sword*. The church contains the tombs of some members of the Bonaparte family and other

The mighty, classical forms of the Dôme des Invalides.

great men of France. In the chapels on the right are the *tombs of Joseph Bonaparte,* and, more northwards, the *tombs of Marshal Foch* and *Marshal Vauban*; in the first chapel on the left is the tomb of Napoleon's other brother, *Jerome,* followed by the tombs of *Turenne* and *Lyautey.*

TOMB OF NAPOLEON – The tomb of the emperor, who died on St Helena on 5 May 1821, is exactly below the centre of the cupola. His body was not brought back to Paris until 1840; on 15 December of that year it was interred here in a ceremony of unequalled solemnity. The body is enclosed in six coffins: the first of tin-sheeted iron, the second of mahogany, the third and fourth of lead, the fifth of ebony, and the sixth of oak. These were then placed in the great red porphyry sarcophagus in the crypt

The porphyry sarcophagus containing the remains of Napoleon.

Auguste Rodin, The Thinker.

designed by Visconti. Here, 12 enormous *Victories* by Pradier keep an eternal vigil. Alongside is the *tomb of Napoleon's son* 'the Eaglet' (l'Aiglon), who died in Vienna in 1832.

MUSÉE RODIN – With its entrance in Rue de Varenne no. 77, the Rodin Museum is in the **Hôtel Biron,** constructed in 1728-1731 by Gabriel and Aubert and the property of Marshal de Biron. In 1820, the building became a convent of the Sacred Heart nuns, where the daughters of the great French families were educated. The Neo-Gothic church in the courtyard, erected under the Mother Superior Sophie Barat, belongs to this period. In 1904 the building was rented to the Victor Duruy Secondary School, and later it was put at the disposal of the sculptor Auguste Rodin, who on his death in 1917 left his works to the State. The museum contains a splendid collection of the great sculptor's works. It has about 500 pieces of sculpture in bronze and white marble. Among the many, we should mention the *Burgher of Calais,* the *Thinker*, and the *statue of Balzac* in the main courtyard, the *Count Ugolino group* in the garden, and the *Kiss* and the *St John the Baptist* in the hall on the ground floor.

6th Itinerary

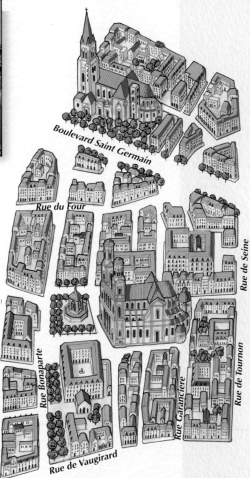

Boulevard Saint Germain

Rue du Four

Rue de Seine

Rue Madame

Rue Bonaparte

Rue Garancière

Rue de Tournon

Rue de Vaugirard

The façade of Palais Bourbon, the meeting-place of the National Assembly.

FAUBOURG ST-GERMAIN – This Left Bank quarter, a suburb built around the Church of St-Germain-des-Prés, is in some respects the aristocratic quarter of Paris: here wealthy burghers, financiers, and aristocrats from Marais built their elegant dwellings with splendid courtyards and vast gardens. These luxurious residences were eventually occupied by embassies and ministries. The decline of the area began under Louis-Philippe and Napoleon III, when the Champs-Élysées gradually took the place of St-Germain.

PALAIS BOURBON

This palace is in front of the Pont de la Concorde (1790), creating a symmetrical relationship with the Madeleine. Today it is the seat of the National Assembly. It is the work of four architects: Giardini began it in 1722, Lassurance continued its construction, and Aubert and Gabriel completed it in 1728. It was originally built for the daughter of Louis XIV, the Duchess of Bourbon, who gave her name to the palace. In 1764 it became the property of the Prince of Condé and was extended to its present dimensions.

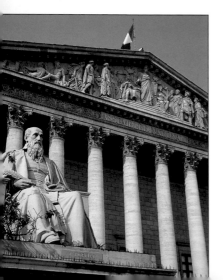

Napoleon had the façade built by Poyet between 1803 and 1807. On the portico is an *allegorical pediment* (Cortot, 1842). The other allegorical bas-reliefs on the wings are by Rude and Pradier.

Interior. It contains a wealth of works of art. In 1838-1845, Delacroix decorated the **Library** with paintings illustrating the *History of Civilisation*. Also in the Library are *busts of Diderot* and *Voltaire*, sculpted by Houdon.

One of the four statues that flank the front stairs and that portray L'Hôpital, Sully, Colbert, and d'Aguesseau.

We now walk along the typical Rue de Lille which, along with Rue de Varenne, Rue Grenelle, and Rue de l'Université, still preserves the spirit of the Faubourg St-Germain of former times.

PALAIS DE LA LÉGION D'HONNEUR – In Rue de Lille no. 64, this building was constructed by the architect Rousseau in 1787 for Prince de Salm and burnt down in 1871 during the period of the Com-

The Pont des Arts with the Institute of France in the background.

mune; it was rebuilt in its original form in 1878. Headquarters since 1804 of the order of the Legion of Honour (instituted by Napoleon in 1802), it has a majestic portal and a colonnaded courtyard. The building houses the **Museum of the Legion of Honour,** containing many relics and documents related to the order created by Napoleon and other European orders of chivalry.

The façade of the Institute of France.

Alongside this building is the **Gare d'Orsay**, the railway station built in 1900 and today home to the Musée d'Orsay. Continuing along the Seine, we reach the picturesque bridge, the **Pont des Arts,** in front of the Louvre: it is the city's first iron bridge, and is now open only to pedestrians.

INSTITUTE OF FRANCE — The building was erected in 1665 as the result of a legacy left by Cardinal Mazarin who in 1661, three days before his death, left 2 million *livres* for the construction of a college to accommodate 60 scholars and to be called the College of the Four Nations. In 1806, Napoleon transferred here the Institute of France, which had been formed in 1795 by the amalgamation of five academies: the Academy of France and the Academies of Science, Belles Lettres, Fine Arts, and Political Sciences. The building was designed by the architect Le Vau, who took his inspiration from the Baroque buildings of Rome. It consists of a central body with a colonnaded façade; the columns support a pediment above which is a fine cupola (on the drum are engraved the insignia of Mazarin). This part is linked to the lateral pavilions by two curving wings, with two orders of pillars. Entering the courtyard we find on the left the **Mazarin Library** and on the right the **Ceremonial Hall.** Here, below the cupola in what was originally the college chapel, the solemn ceremony for the presentation of new members of the French Academy takes place. The vestibule preceding the hall

The exterior of the Café de Flore,
one of St-Germain's most characteristic
meeting-places.

contains the *tomb of
Mazarin* (Coysevox, 1689).

LA MONNAIE - The Mint
(La Monnaie) is at no. 11
Quai de Conti, next to the
Institute. Its imposing building was constructed in
1771-1777 by the architect
Antoine. The façade, more
than 117 metres long, is
simple in line, with three
orders of windows and a
projecting central body
with colonnade. Inside, a
monumental stairway leads up to the **Museum of the Mint,**
with its collections of coins and medals ancient and modern.

PLACE ST-GERMAIN-DES-PRÉS - Passing through the tiny
streets typical of this quarter, full of antiquarians and art
merchants, we reach this square, the heart of old Paris
and a meeting place for the Left Bank intellectuals.
The cafés and brasseries that animate the square have
been, over the years, the witnesses of the birth of many
of the literary, philosophical, and artistic movements
that marked the history of the 1900s.
Rimbaud and Picasso sat in the *Café des Deux
Magots;* at the *Café de Flore,* also patronized by
Jean Cocteau, Jean Genet, and Boris Vian, Jean-
Paul Sartre and Simone de Beauvoir lay down the
ground rules for what was to come to be known
as Existentialism. In the smoky atmosphere of
the nearby *caves,* the 'muse' Juliette Greco, her
long hair let down, wearing a black turtle-
neck, brought the poetic verses of Brassens
and Léo Ferré to the attention of the

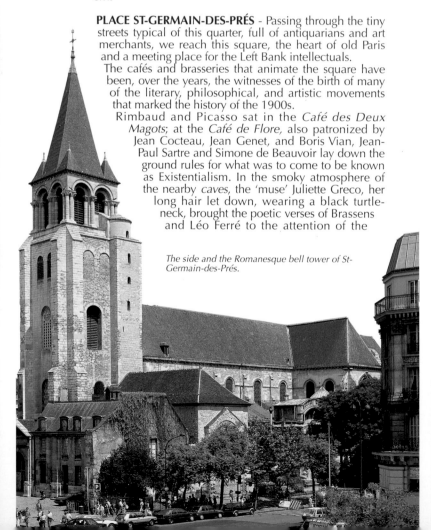

The side and the Romanesque bell tower of St-
Germain-des-Prés.

world. On the other side of the avenue, at the *Brasserie Lipp*, Paul Valéry, Max Jacob, Léon Blum, and Girardoux met to discuss their respective points of view.

ST-GERMAIN-DES-PRÉS

A rare example of Romanesque architecture in Paris, St-Germain is the city's oldest church. It was erected in the 11th and 12th centuries, and though devastated no less than four times in forty years by the Normans it was rebuilt each time in its severe Romanesque forms. In front of it are the remains of the 12th-century portal, half-hidden by the 17th-century porch which was erected in 1607. The bell tower, on the other hand, is completely Romanesque, with its corners strengthened by robust buttresses.

Interior. It has three aisles and a transept, the end of which was modified in the 17th century. The chancel and ambulatory still retain much of the original 12th-century architecture. In the second chapel on the right is the *tomb of the great philosopher Descartes,* and in the left transept that of the Polish king *John Casimir.*

On the left side of the church, in front of Rue de l'Abbaye, is the tiny Rue de Furstenberg: at no. 6 is the house where Eugène Delacroix died in 1863. Today the house contains the painter's personal effects. Not far from St-Germain, in a quarter where there are many shops selling religious objects and sacred images, is Place St-Sulpice, with the church of the same name.

ST-SULPICE

St-Sulpice is the largest church in Paris after Notre-Dame. Six architects directed its construction over a period of 134 years. The last of these, the Florentine G. N. Servandoni, erected the imposing façade, though it was later partly modified by Maclaurin and Chalgrin. Today it consists of a double portico surmounted by a loggia with balcony and flanked by two towers. The façades of the transept at the sides of the church have two orders, one above the other, in the Jesuit style.

Two images of St-Sulpice.

Interior. It is impressive and grandiose: 110 metres long, 56 wide, and 33 high (thus larger than, but not so high as, St-Eustache). Above the entrance is one of the finest organs in France, designed by Chalgrin in 1776 and reconstructed in 1862 by Cavaillé-Coll. The two *holywater stoups* against the first pillars of the nave are giant shells given to François I by the Republic of Venice and donated to the church by Louis XV in 1745. The splendid frescoes in the first chapel on the right, full of Romantic vigour, were painted by Eugène Delacroix between 1849 and 1861. On the right wall, *Heliodorus Driven from the Temple,* on the left, *Jacob Struggling with the Angel,* and in the vault, *St Michael Slaying the Dragon.* Two statues by Bouchardon, *Our Lady of the Sorrows* and *Christ against the Pillar,* adorn the pillars in the chancel. In the Lady Chapel, decoration of which was supervised by Servandoni, there is a *Virgin and Child* by Pigalle in the niche above the alter, plus canvases by Van Loo on the walls and a fresco by Lemoyne in the dome.

LES CARMES – At no. 70 Rue de Vaugirard, this is the ancient monastery of the Barefoot Carmelites, founded in 1611. It is an infamous site, because here, on 2 September 1792, 115 monks were massacred without pity, guilty of not have taken the oath specified by the Civil Constitution for the Clergy. The tomb of the victims is in the crypt.

LUXEMBOURG

Rue de Vaugirard takes us directly to the main point of interest in this quarter, the Luxembourg Palace, surrounded by its famous garden.

The elegant façade of the Luxembourg Palace.

PALACE – Its construction was due to Marie de' Medici who, after the death of King Henri IV, decided to live not in the Louvre but in a place which in some way reminded her of Florence, the city from which she came. In 1612 she acquired the mansion of Duke François of Luxembourg, with its extensive grounds, and in 1615 commissioned Salomon de Brosse to erect a palace, the style and materials of which were to be as similar as possible to those of the Florentine palaces she had left to come to France. And in fact the building's rustication and large ringed columns recall the Palazzo Pitti in Florence more than any other palace in Paris. The façade consists of a pavilion with two orders covered by a cupola, with two wings at the sides linked to the central building by galleries. When the Revolution broke out, the palace was taken from

The Medici Fountain, attributed to Salomon de Brosse.

the royal family and converted into a State prison. On 4 November 1795, the First Directory adopted it as its seat, and Napoleon later used it as the Senate's chambers. To visit the interior of the palace, permission from the Secretary-General of the Senate is needed. The Library is decorated with celebrated pictures painted by Delacroix in 1847 (*Dante and Virgil in Limbo, Alexander Placing Homer's Poems in the Casket of Darius*), and on the ceiling of the Gallery are the *Signs of the Zodiac*, painted by Jordaens.

GARDENS – Covering no less than 23 hectares, the gardens are a public park frequented every day by students from the Latin Quarter. Among the trees one can find fountains, groups of statues, and even playing fields. A fine series of statues depicting the queens of France and illustrious women lines the terraces of the park. At the end of a canal on the eastern side of the palace, framed by the greenery, is the splendid **Medici Fountain,** attributed to Salomon de Brosse. In the central niche is depicted *Polyphemus Surprising Galatea with the Shepherd Acis,* by Ottin (1863). On the back is a bas-relief of *Leda and the Swan* done by Valois in 1806.

PETIT LUXEMBOURG – This is on the right of the Luxembourg Palace, with its entrance at no. 17 Rue de Vaugirard. Once the property of Marie de' Medici and of Cardinal Richelieu, it is now occupied by the President of the Senate.

AVENUE DE L'OBSERVATOIRE – This is a splendid avenue lined with trees, which runs from the Luxembourg Gardens to the Observatory. In the middle of the avenue, surrounded by greenery, is the celebrated fountain called the *Fountain of the Four Parts of the*

World (Davioud, 1875). It has a group of maidens who symbolise the four parts of the world, sculpted with extraordinary lightness and grace by Carpeaux.

OBSERVATORY – At the end of the avenue is the Observatory, seat of the International Time Bureau since 1919. Construction of the Observatory, designed by Claude Perrault, was begun by order of Colbert on 21 June 1667 (the day of the summer solstice). The four walls of the building are oriented exactly to the four cardinal points of the compass, and the Paris meridian of longitude passes exactly through the building's centre.

From here one reaches **Place Denfert-Rochereau,** the square which takes its name from the colonel who fiercely opposed the

The Observatory fountain, also called the Fountain of the Four Parts of the World.

Francis Scott Fitzgerald.

Amedeo Modigliani.

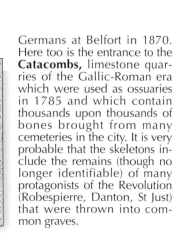

Germans at Belfort in 1870. Here too is the entrance to the **Catacombs,** limestone quarries of the Gallic-Roman era which were used as ossuaries in 1785 and which contain thousands upon thousands of bones brought from many cemeteries in the city. It is very probable that the skeletons include the remains (though no longer identifiable) of many protagonists of the Revolution (Robespierre, Danton, St Just) that were thrown into common graves.

MONTPARNASSE

The name Montparnasse derives from a small hill, familiarly called Mount Parnassus, which was levelled during the 18th century. During the years between 1920 and 1940, the quarter was frequented above all by artists, writers, and painters, who gave Montparnasse its typically Bohemian atmosphere, making it the companion and rival of the other celebrated quarter of Montmartre. Among its inhabitants have been painters like Amedeo Modigliani, fascinating and 'damned', who lived in the quarter until his death, and Picasso, who worked both here and at the Bateau-Lavoir of Montmartre.

The area between Boulevard Montparnasse, Boulevard Raspail, and Rue de Rennes is the liveliest in Montparnasse.

Like Saint-Germain, Montparnasse too has its 'historic' spots: *La Closerie des Lilas*, with its lovely Art Déco interior; *La Rotonde*, which was patronized by Trotsky, among others; *Le Dôme*, on the other side of the avenue; *La Coupole*, with its restaurant with 24 decorated pillars. And nearby, the *Sélect*, the first bar in Paris to be open all night.These were the habitual haunts of the small colony of Americans that counted among its numbers Hemingway, Scott Fitzgerald, and Henry Miller; those Americans defined by Gertrude Stein (who lived in Rue de Fleurus) as 'the lost generation'. Hemingway wrote his *The Sun Also Rises* (British title, *Fiesta*) at a table at La Coupole. The heart and nerve centre of the area is **Carrefour Raspail,** the crossroads where Boulevard Raspail and Boulevard Montparnasse meet. Here stands one of Rodin's finest works, the bronze representing *Balzac*, 2.8 metres high, done in 1897.

CEMETERY – This is one of the most interesting places in the area to visit. Built in 1824, in it are buried writers (*Proudhon, Maupassant, Huysmans, Baudelaire*), painters (*Fantin-Latour, Soutine*), sculptors (*Brancusi, Rude, Houdon, Tristan Tzara*), composers (*Franck, Saint-Saëns*) and *Captain Dreyfus*, protagonist and victim of the famous 'Dreyfus Affair'.

Despite the many building constructions which have changed the quarter's appearance, making it much more modern, Montparnasse nevertheless preserves many signs of its artistically rich past. At no. 16 Rue Bourdelle is the **Bourdelle Museum,** which contains almost all the works done by the sculptor Antoine Bourdelle (sculpture, paintings, drawings). Montparnasse also contains a rare example of the technique of metal construction applied to a religious building: the Church of **Notre-Dame-du-Travail,** built in 1900. Further on, we come to Rue de la Gaîté, so called because in the 18th century it was lined by restaurants, cabarets, and dance halls. At no. 20 today is the **Bobino,** a famous music hall.

7th Itinerary

THE LATIN QUARTER

The Latin Quarter has become synonymous with the Sorbonne University. An extremely old part of Paris, it became its scholarly centre in the 13th century when the University was moved from the Île de la Cité to the Left Bank. The University quickly gained fame because students were attracted by the great masters who taught there (St Bonaventure, St Thomas Aquinas, St Albert the Great). Our itinerary through the Latin Quarter can begin from **Place St-Michel,** dating from the time of Napoleon III. Its fine **fountain** (Davioud, 1860) is adorned by the bronze group of *St Michael Slaying the Dragon*. In this square, in August 1944, bitter fighting took place between the students of the Resistance and the Germans.

The Latin Quarter was also the theatre of the student uprisings of May 1968: in the night of 11-12 May, demonstrators expelled from the Sorbonne erected numerous barricades in the quarter and were involved in angry skirmishes with the police.

The fountain by Davioud in Place St-Michel.

The Latin Quarter

Rue Saint Jacques

Rue Valette

Place du Panthéon

Rue des Fosses Saint Jacques

Rue Descartes

Rue Pierre et Marie Curie

Rue de l'Estrapade

Rue d'Ulm

Rue Jourrelort

Rue P. Brossolette

Rue Rataud

Rue Vauquelin

The Panthéon seen from Place Rostand.

BOULEVARD ST-MICHEL – This wide avenue, built during the Second Empire and familiarly called by the Parisians 'Boul' Mich', ascends from the Seine towards the hill of Ste Geneviève. Animated by its new and secondhand bookshops, noisy cafés, exotic restaurants, and avant-garde cinemas, it is the heart of the quarter.

ST-SÉVERIN – From as early as the end of the 11th century, St-Séverin was the parish church of the whole Left Bank. Construction of the church as we see it today lasted from the first half of the 13th century until the end of the 16th. The **portal** of the façade, dating from the 13th century, comes from the Church of St-Pierre-aux-Bœufs, demolished in 1839. The windows and rose window above it are in the Flamboyant Gothic style of the 15th century, while the bell tower standing on the left is from the 13th century. Small sculpted cusps run along the sides and around the apse of the church. The **interior,** 50 metres long, 34 metres wide, and 17 metres high, has five aisles, no transept, and a small chancel. The first three bays of the nave are the oldest, belonging to the 13th century, while the others date from the 15th and 16th centuries. Above the arcades is the triforium gallery, the oldest in Paris. The pillars in the first bays are adorned with capitals, unlike those of the following bays, which are in the Flamboyant Gothic style. The **apse** has five arcades which are higher than those in the chancel. Admirable in the chancel is the splendid double ambulatory, erected between 1489 and 1494, with its multiple rib tracery radiating out from the top of the columns. The windows have beautiful stained glass from the end of the 15th century. The stained-glass window in the façade illustrates the *Tree of Jesse* (early 16th century).

A decorative element in Square René Viviani.

The apse of St-Séverin.

The façade of the ancient church of St-Julien-le-Pauvre.

ST-JULIEN-LE-PAUVRE – Although small, this church is extremely picturesque. It is one of the oldest churches in Paris, its construction dating back to the same period as that of Notre-Dame (from about 1165 to 1220). Since 1889 it has been a Catholic church of the Malachite rite. The structure of the church was considerably modified in the 17th century, when two bays of the nave and the façade were demolished.

SQUARE RENÉ VIVIANI – This small garden, planted with lime-trees, stands in front of the church. Here, in 1620, a Robinia tree was planted: introduced from North America by the botanist Robin, from whom it took its name, the tree is now one of the oldest in Paris. The view of the side of Notre-Dame from here is perhaps the finest in the city.

HÔTEL DE CLUNY

This building, standing in its green garden, is without doubt one of the finest examples of Flamboyant Gothic architecture. The *hôtel* stands on the site of the ruins of the Roman baths, dating from the 2nd or early 3rd century. The site was the property of the Abbey of Cluny in Burgundy and on it, between 1485 and 1498, Abbot Jacques d'Amboise had a building constructed to accommodate the Benedictine monks who came from Cluny to visit the capital. During the Revolution it became the property of the State and was sold, becoming in 1833 the residence of the collector Alexandre du Sommerard. On his death in 1842, both the building and the collections it contained passed to the State. In 1844 the museum was opened; it contains objects which illustrate the life of medieval France, including costumes, arms, goldsmiths' works, ceramics, tapestries, paintings, and statues.

Two examples of the Flamboyant Gothic style of the Hôtel de Cluny.

MUSÉE NATIONALE DU MOYEN ÂGE

MUSÉE NATIONALE DU MOYEN ÂGE - Entrance to the museum is from the courtyard. From here the whole building can be admired in all its beauty: it has two orders of cross windows and a tower containing a staircase, ornamented with the emblems of St James. The balustrade on the roof and the dormer windows are typical of the Flamboyant Gothic style.

The Museum consists of 24 rooms. One of its most precious collections is the one of tapestries woven in the Loire and in Flanders in the 15th and 16th centuries. Room XIII, also called the Rotunda, contains the famous series of tapestries of the *Lady and the Unicorn,* from the early 16th century. On this floor, the most famous room is without doubt Room XX, the **Chapelle,** the ancient oratory of the abbots. In pure Flamboyant Gothic style, it has a single pillar in the centre, from which the ribs of the vault fan out; along the walls is a series of niches on consoles, containing the statues of the d'Amboise family. In this chapel are the celebrated tapestries illustrating the *Legend of St Stephen,* woven for the cathedral of Auxerre and completed towards 1490. In Room XIV is another early 16th century tapestry depicting the *Parable of the Prodigal Son.*

ÉCOLE DE MÉDECINE – The School of Medicine, at no. 12 in picturesque Rue de l'École de Médecine, was constructed between 1769 and 1786. Its enlargement in 1878-1900 led to the demolition of historic buildings including the house where Charlotte Corday stabbed Marat to death and the studio where Courbet worked. In front of the building is a *statue of Danton* (A. Paris, 1891).

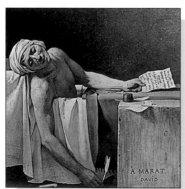

COLLÈGE DE FRANCE – The Collège de France was created in 1530 by François I as a place of learning independent from the Sorbonne. Since 1852 it has been dependent on the Ministry for National Education, but independent

The delicate Gothic ribbing of the ceiling of the Chapelle of the Hôtel de Cluny.

Jacques-Louis David, Marat Assassinated.

The façade of the church of the Sorbonne,
with its typically Baroque forms, and a
detail of the sculptures on the tympanum.

courses of literature and scientific subjects are given here. In
front of it is a garden in which are a *statue of Dante* (Aubé,
1879) and a monument representing the *Pleiades*. In an underground laboratory is the cyclotron with which Frédéric Joliot-
Curie achieved the fission of the uranium nucleus.

SORBONNE – The name Sorbonne indicates the complex of
buildings which the University of Paris has occupied for seven
centuries. In 1253 the confessor of King Louis IX, Robert de
Sorbon, founded a college in which theology was also taught to
poorer students, and this was the original nucleus of what was
to be the famous university. In the vast area which it occupies
today are the various institutes and lecture rooms, besides other
parts such as the library and the chancellor's lodge.

CHURCH OF THE SORBONNE – This is the oldest part of the
university buildings; erected between 1635 and 1642 by
Lemercier, it has a typically Baroque façade with two orders,
surmounted and dominated by its elegant cupola. Volutes link
the lower order to the upper. The columns at ground level become flatter pilaster strips higher up, thus gradually accentuat-
ing the luminous quality of the structure. In the **interior**, the
white marble *tomb of Cardinal Richelieu,* sculpted by Girardon
in 1694 to a design by Le Brun, dominates the transept.

The hill on which we are now is called the Montagne Ste-Geneviève. We walk along Rue Soufflot, full of bookshops and publishers of legal works. At the top of the street, at the corner of Place du Panthéon, are on the left the **Faculty of Law** (Soufflot, 1770) and on the right the **Town Hall of the 5th Arrondissement** (Hittorf, 1850). In the square, which is dominated by the majestic mass of the Panthéon, is the **Library of Ste-Geneviève,** designed by Labrouste (1844-1850), with a wealth of manuscripts and early printed books. At the sides of the Panthéon are two marble statues, representing *Corneille* and *Rousseau*.

PANTHÉON

Born as the Church of Ste-Geneviève because of a vow made in 1744 by Louis XV when he was seriously ill, the Panthéon was designed by Soufflot in 1758 and completed under the supervision of Rondelet in 1789. During the Revolution, it became the Temple of Fame, in which the nation's great men were buried. Napoleon reopened it for worship in 1806, but this lasted only until 1885, when it reverted once and for all to its status as a secular temple. Its dimensions are

The tomb of Voltaire in the Panthéon.

The sedate, classical façade of the Panthéon.

exceptional: 110 metres long by 83 metres high. A stairway in front of the temple leads up to a pronaos with 22 columns, supporting a pediment on which in 1831 David d'Angers sculpted the allegorical work representing the *Nation between Liberty and History*. Here can also be read the celebrated inscription: '*Aux grands hommes, la patrie reconnaissante* ('To the great men, from their grateful fatherland'). The great dome, its drum surrounded by a portico of Corinthian columns, dominates the whole building.

Interior. In the form of a Greek cross; the dome above the crossing is supported by four pillars. On the walls are the *Stories of Ste Geneviève*, painted by Puvis de Chavannes.

The Panthéon is the final resting place of many great men. Jean-Jacques Rousseau was buried here in 1794; Victor Hugo's remains were transferred here in 1885; Émile Zola, Voltaire, Carnot, Mirabeau, and the designer of the building Soufflot are also buried here. André Malraux was entombed here in 1996.

There are 425 steps leading up to the dome, from which there is a vast and impressive panoramic view.

ST-ÉTIENNE-DU-MONT

This is one of the most unusual churches in Paris, because of both its façade and the interior. It was begun in 1492 but completed only in 1622. The façade is a bizarre amalgamation of Gothic and Renaissance styles, with three superimposed pediments.

Views of the exterior and interior of the remarkable church of St-Étienne-du-Mont.

Interior. The inside is also extremely unusual. In Gothic style with three aisles and transept, it has very high cylindrical piers supporting the vaulting, linked by a tribune running above the arcades. But the most interesting part of the church is the *jubé*, the rood loft that separates the nave from the chancel. It was possibly designed by Philibert Delorme and is the only existing *jubé* in Paris; it was erected between 1521 and 1545. Its rich openwork of Renaissance inspiration continues in the two spiral staircases at the sides. In the ambulatory, alongside the pillars of the Lady Chapel, are the *tombs of Pascal* and *of Racine*. The church also has fine stained glass from the 16th and 17th centuries.

St-Étienne also contains the *Shrine of Ste Geneviève*, patron saint of Paris, who in 451 saved the city from the menace of the Huns.

VAL-DE-GRÂCE

Construction of this splendid architectural complex in the 17th century was due to Anne of Austria, who at the age of 38 had not yet had any children and made a vow to construct a magnificent church if she should finally give birth to an heir. In 1638 the future Louis XIV was born, and work on the church was begun immediately to the plans prepared by François Mansart. In 1645 the young king himself laid the foundation stone. But the queen decided that Mansart was too slow and appointed Le Mercier to take his place. Yet another architect, Le Duc, completed the church in 1667. It was consecrated in 1710. Constructed in the Jesuit style, Val-de-Grâce has a façade with two orders of columns and double superimposed triangular pediments. Above these, in turn, is the beautiful, slender cupola, 40 metres high.

Interior. The interior is in the purest Baroque style: without aisles, with barrel vaulting, linking chapels on the sides, and a chancel with six chapels (two on the sides and four in the corners). The cupola is adorned by a grandiose fresco by P. Mignard, depicting the *Glory of the Elect,* in which there are over 200 figures three times larger than life-size. The sculptural decoration is the work of Anguier and Philippe Buyster. On the right is the **St Louis Chapel,** the former chancel of the Benedictines; on the left, the **St Anne Chapel,** in which from 1662 the hearts of the royal and Orléans families were placed, though they disappeared in 1792 during the Revolution. Of the former Benedictine monastery which stood here, the fine **cloister** with its two orders of galleries and the pavilion where Anne of Austria stayed can still be seen today.

ST-MÉDARD – The church stands at the end of Rue Monge, in front of the colourful and lively Rue Mouffetard. Dedicated to St Médard, the counsellor of the Merovingian kings, it was begun in the 15th century and not completed until 1655. The façade is set with a great Flamboyant Gothic window; the nave inside is in the same style, while the chancel is in Renaissance style. The church contains some interesting works of art, including a *St Joseph and the Christ Child* attributed to Zurbarán and a *Dead Christ* by Philippe de Champaigne.

GOBELINS' TAPESTRY FACTORY – The Manufacture des Gobelins, famous throughout the world, is at no. 42 Avenue des Gobelins. A dyer called Jean Gobelin set up his small workshop in this building in 1440. In 1601 it was sold by his descendants to two Flemish tapestry workers, summoned to Paris from Brussels by King Henri IV. Then, in 1662, Louis XIV ordered Colbert to group the city's various dying shops together here, thus creating the 'Royal Factory of Tapestry-Makers to the Crown', to which five years later the Royal Cabinet-Makers were added. More than 5,000 tapestries of great value have been woven here to the cartoons of the great masters (Poussin, Van Loo, Boucher, and even Picasso). The craftsmen's methods and organisation in the factory have remained unchanged since the 17th century. Both the workshops and the gallery, where tapestries of the 17th and 18th centuries are exhibited, can be visited. The museum, in stone and brick, was built by Jean-Camille Formigé between 1912 and 1918.

At the end of Avenue des Gobelins opens the circular **Place d'Italie**, the site of the ancient customshouse of Paris and today the centre of a lively, fast-developing quarter. From here, along Boulevard Vincent Auriol, we come to that which is considered Paris' most important development work of the early 2000s; that is, the **Seine-Rive Gauche quarter**, with the new **Charles de Gaulle bridge**, the city's thirty-seventh, in the form of an aeroplane aileron, and above all with the new premises of the French National Library.

BIBLIOTHÈQUE NATIONALE DE FRANCE – Although it was officially inaugurated on 17 December 1996 by Jacques Chirac, the Library was actually the pet project of Chirac's predecessor François Mitterrand, who tenaciously promoted its advancement during his second mandate.
The new Bibliothèque Nationale de France, which the Parisians prefer calling 'TGB' (abbreviation of *Très Grande Bibliothèque*, assonant with the tag given the high-speed TGV train), rises in the Tolbiac quarter. It was designed by the architect Dominique Perrault, and occupies an area of about eight hectares. The four towers, one at each corner, each eighty metres in height, resemble open books - and in fact contain books. The Library's more than 12 million volumes come from the old library premises in Rue Richelieu, which is nevertheless still the home of the manuscripts and the most precious and rarest editions.

The inner courtyard of the Salpêtrière, theatre of grievous episodes during the French Revolution.

On one of the avenues in the Jardin des Plantes, the statue of Bernardin de Saint-Pierre by Charles Eugène Potron.

Beyond Boulevard Vincent Auriol is the largest healthcare complex in the city, the **Salpêtrière Hospital**. Originally a place where gunpowder was made from saltpetre, it was converted into a hospital by Louis XIV in 1684. In front of the huge and imposing building is a vast Italian garden. In the centre is the octagonal dome of the **St Louis Chapel,** surmounted by a lantern. The interior is original in form: four aisles surrounding a rotunda to form a Greek cross. The young Freud studied in the Salpêtrière Hospital under the guidance of Charcot. Boulevard de l'Hôpital ends at the **Pont d'Austerlitz** in Place Valhubert, on one side of which is the railway station called the **Gare d'Austerlitz,** built in 1869. In front of the bridge is the main entrance to the Jardin des Plantes.

JARDIN DES PLANTES – The Jardin des Plantes, or Botanical Garden, dates back to 1626, when Hérouard and Guy de la Brosse, the doctors of Louis XIII, established the Royal Garden of Medicinal Herbs, opened to the public in 1650. Its collections of plants were enriched by Louis XIV's first doctor, Fagon, by the botanist Tournefort, by the three Jussieu brothers, who travelled the world in search of new plants, and above all by the great naturalist Buffon; the latter made the greatest contribution to the gardens, enlarging them as far as the Seine and building the galleries, the maze, and the amphitheatre. At the time of the Revolution, the gardens came to house the National Museum of Natural History. As a result of the work of many eminent scholars, this has become one of the richest museums of its type in the world.

Visit to the gardens. After passing through the gate, we reach the **Botanical Garden,** its vast flower beds divided by wide paths. Here are the **School of Botany,** containing more than 10,000 species of plants, all methodically classified; the **Winter Garden,** with tropical plants; the **Alpine Garden,** with collections of plants from the polar regions, the Himalaya Mountains, and the Alps.

MUSEUM OF NATURAL HISTORY – This is on the other side of the path on the left and contains various sections: *Palaeontology* (fossils, prehistoric animals, casts of extinct species),

Botany, Mineralogy (precious stones, minerals, meteorites) and the *hunting collections of the Duke of Orléans.* In the *Zoology* gallery are skeletons, shells, and lifelike stuffed animals. Near this gallery, on the other side of the *Glasshouses* (containing plants from South America, Australia, etc.), is the *Maze* with its rare plants, including the cedar of Lebanon planted in 1734 by Bernard de Jussieu. Also worth visiting are the *Ménageries,* with birds and wild animals, elephants, monkeys, and so on.

MOSQUE – Near the gardens, with its entrance in Place du Puits-de-l'Ermite, is the Mosque, an unusual corner of the Orient here in the middle of the ancient heart of Paris which cannot fail to attract the tourist's attention. The Mosque has an interesting **courtyard** in Hispano-Moorish style, a **patio** inspired by that of the Alhambra at Granada, and a **prayer chamber** adorned with precious carpets. It was built between 1922 and 1926.

ARÈNES DE LUTÈCE (Lutetia Arena) – With its entrance at no. 49 Rue Monge, this is the Roman arena of the ancient city. The exact date of the construction of this Gallic-Roman monument is not known, though it was probably in the 2nd or 3rd century. It was destroyed by the barbarians in 280 and rediscovered only in 1869. At the beginning of the 20th century, it was restored and opened as a park. The arena had the functions of an amphitheatre, where circus games took place, and also of a theatre. The seating section was elliptical in form, with 36 rows of seats, many of which are now lost.

ST-NICOLAS-DU-CHARDONNET – Dedicated to St Nicholas, patron saint of boatmen, it was built in the Baroque style between 1656 and 1709. On the exterior, note the outstanding side door carved from wood after a design by Le Brun. The **interior**, in the Jesuit style, has three naves with chancel and ambulatory, and contains many works of art. In the first chapel on the right, a work by Corot depicting the *Baptism of Jesus;* in the ambulatory, in the second chapel on the right, the *funeral monument to the Solicitor General Jérôme Bignon* by Girardon.

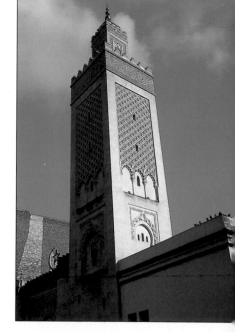

The minaret of the mosque of Paris, a copy of that of Fez, soars to 26 meters.

8th Itinerary

PLACE DE L'HÔTEL DE VILLE – Its present appearance dates from 1853, but for many centuries, from 1310 to 1830, this vast area was the site of public executions (in 1721 the brigand Cartouche was put to death here). Flanked by the Rue de Rivoli on one side and the Seine on the other, it is dominated by the wide façade of the Hôtel de Ville.

HÔTEL DE VILLE

The illustrious old Hôtel de Ville, today the seat of the city's municipal government, stands on the site previously occupied by a 16th-century building designed by Domenico da Cortona and built in the Renaissance style but destroyed by fire at the time of the Commune in 1871. The present building was inspired by the previous one. Designed by Deperthes and Ballu, it was completed in 1882. It consists of several pavilions surmounted by domes in the form of truncated pyramids, with a forest of statues in every possible position. There are 136 on the building's four façades, including one, on a terrace, depicting Étienne Marcel, leader of the Parisian merchants and fomenter of the disorders which crippled Paris in the 14th century. Inside the building, on 27 July 1794, the soldiers of the Convention arrested Robespierre and his followers.

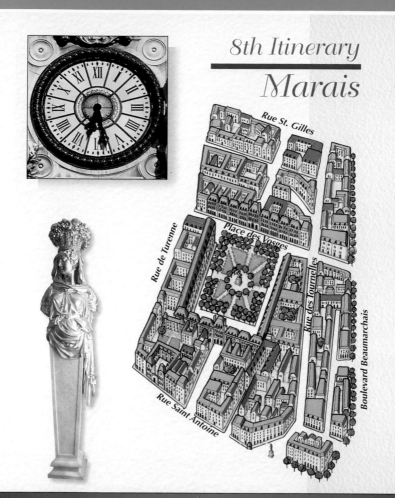

8th Itinerary
Marais

Rue St. Gilles

Rue de Turenne

Place des Vosges

Rue des Tournelles

Boulevard Beaumarchais

Rue Saint Antoine

ST-GERVAIS - ST-PROTAIS –

The church of St-Gervais-St-Protais in an old engraving.

Dedicated to St Gervase and St Protase, two brothers martyred under Nero, the church stands on a small square behind the Hôtel de Ville. The Flamboyant Gothic building was begun in 1494 and completed in 1657. The **façade** is an imposing example of Classicism (the first in Paris) and was erected between 1616 and 1621 by Métezeau (or by Salomon de Brosse, according to another theory by critics): it has three orders of columns in the Doric, Ionic, and Corinthian styles. In the **interior** are three naves supported by pillars, with a transept, choir, ambulatory, and side chapels. Over the central nave and the choir are beautiful 16th-century stained-glass windows, and over the center portal an organ built in 1601. There are also many works of art: a painting by Sebastiano Ricci, the *tomb of Marcel Le Tellier* (Chancellor under Louis XIV), and a fine altar-facing of the *Death of the Virgin*.

In the **Chapelle Dorée**, dated 1628, precious painted panels are set in the wooden wainscotting; up against a pillar, a Gothic *Virgin with Child* in polychrome stone.

RUE DES ARCHIVES – This street, running from Rue de Rivoli to the Square du Temple, belonged to the old aristocratic **quarter of Marais,** which became very fashionable at the beginning of the 17th century. In fact this was the birthplace of the typical French *hôtel,* a Classical mansion with garden and courtyard. But when high society moved to the more fashionable areas of Île-St-Louis and later St-Germain, the quarter's decline set in and it was completely abandoned with the taking of the Bastille. Today the Marais quarter, after having been the object of an extraordinary architectural and urbanistic relaunch, is once again the 'parlour' of Paris.

At no. 22 Rue des Archives is the **Billettes Church** (1756), and at the following number the only medieval cloister left in Paris can be visited. Further on, at no. 60, is the **Hôtel Guénégaud,** built between 1648 and 1651 by François Mansart and reconstructed in the 18th century: simple and sober in form, it contains the **Museum of the Hunt**.

NATIONAL ARCHIVES – These are the most important buildings in the street and the richest archives in the world: a collection of 6 billion documents related to the history of France from the Merovingian era to our own times. The archives today are contained in the **Hôtel de Soubise** and the **Hôtel de Rohan.**

HÔTEL DE SOUBISE – Entrance to the building is at no. 60 Rue des Francs-Bourgeois: from the courtyard, which has a horseshoe shape, the façade with the *statues of the Seasons* can be admired. On the first floor are the splendid apartments of the Prince and Princess of Soubise, with frescoes by the finest painters and works by the finest sculptors of the era (Boucher, Van Loo, Lemoyne, Adam, and others). Here is the **Historical Museum of France,** in which many documents are displayed. Among them are the acts of foundation of the Sainte-Chapelle and the Sorbonne, the Edict of Nantes and its later Revocation, one of the six letters written by Joan of Arc, the first catalogue of the Louvre Museum, dated 10 August 1793, and Napoleon's will.

PICASSO MUSEUM

This museum, inaugurated in 1985, is situated in Rue de Thorigny in the Hôtel Salé, built in 1656 by J. Boullier for Aubert de Fontenay, a tax collector (hence the building's nickname).

The entrance to the Picasso Museum in the Hôtel Salé.

Here is the famous exhibit of 'Picasso's Picassos'; that is, the sculptures and paintings from which the great Spanish artist, who died in 1973, never wanted to be separated. There are over 200 paintings, 158 sculptures, 88 ceramics, over three thousand engravings and sketches, and an incredible number of letters, objects, photographs, and manuscripts. Then there is Picasso's personal collection, previously at the Louvre: there are works by Cézanne, Renoir, Braque, Modigliani, and Matisse. Amongst the numerous works exhibited are *Self-Portrait in Blue* (1901), the *Three Women under a Tree,* painted between 1907 and 1908, the *Great Nude in the Red Armchair,* the *Crucifixion* (1930), and the *Composition with Butterfly,* painted in 1932 and until recently thought to have disappeared. All of these works were given to the French State by the heirs of the Spanish genius as payment for succession duties on the properties owned in France by Picasso.

HÔTEL DE ROHAN – The entrance is at no. 87 Rue Vieille-du-Temple; the building is linked to the Palais Soubise by a garden, which the main façade overlooks. In the courtyard on the right, above the former stables, are the magnificent *Horses of Apollo,* a masterpiece by Robert Le Lorrain. A stairway leads up to the apartments on the first floor. Among the most interesting parts are the luxurious *Gilded Hall* and the original *Monkey Room,* decorated by Huet (1749-1752).

RUE DES FRANCS-BOURGEOIS – This is the other important street in this quarter. In 1334, the *maisons d'aumône,* or almshouses, were founded here, a place of refuge for poor citizens who paid no tax, which is what 'francs-bourgeois' means. Along this street too, which runs from Rue des Archives to Place des Vosges, are the mansions of the aristocrats. At no. 53 is the back entrance to **Notre-Dame-des-Blancs-Manteaux** (a church with a splendid *wooden pulpit* with ivory inlays, a Flemish work done in 1749 in the Rococo style). Also interesting is the **Hôtel Hérouet,** the home of Jean Hérouet, treasurer of king Louis XIII, with its elegant octagonal turret built in 1510. At no. 31 is the **Hôtel d'Albret,** built in the 16th century but restored in the 17th, with a fine façade reconstructed in the 18th century. Further along, at the corner of Rue Pavée, is the **Hôtel de Lamoignon.** Built in 1580 for Diane of France, the legitimised daughter of Henri II, in 1658 it became the residence of Lamoignon, president of Paris' first Parliament. Alphonse Daudet also lived there in the 19th century.

The main body of the building is divided by six Corinthian pilasters, and the façade overlooks the courtyard. Here too is the **Historical Library of the City of Paris**.

HÔTEL CARNAVALET – The entrance to this *hôtel*, home to one of the city's most interesting museums, is at no. 23 Rue de Sévigné. The Museum occupies two buildings linked by a corridor: the Hôtel Carnavalet and the Hôtel Le Peletier de Saint-Fargeau. The first, considered to be one of Paris' most beautiful, was built in 1544 in Renaissance style and embellished by the lovely raised decoration of Jean Goujon; it was remodelled in 1655 by François Mansart, who added a floor and thus gave it the look it still has today. In 1677, the building was rented by the writer Marie de Rabutin, better known as the Marquise de Sévigné. In the 19th century the Museum was opened. It contains historical documents of great importance and rarity related to the history of Paris, from Henri IV to our own time, as seen through its historical figures, monuments, and costumes.

Passing through the main entrance (16th century; the *lions* and the *cornucopia* on the keystone were carved by Jean Goujon), we reach the courtyard, in the centre of which is the *bronze statue of Louis XIV,* by Coysevox (1689).

The Hôtel Carnavalet as it looked in the mid-18th century.

One of the building's inner courtyards.

The building at the end is still in Gothic style, while the *reliefs of the Four Seasons* are Renaissance, the work of the school of Goujon.

CARNAVALET MUSEUM

The entrance to the museum is from the courtyard, on the right.

Rooms 1 through 4 are dedicated to the first centuries of the history of Paris, from the Gallic-Roman era to the late Middle Ages (don't miss the *Treasure of Nanterre*). There follow six rooms illustrating the city of the 16th century, with many views of Paris, including a *Réunion Galante* of the Flemish school and a *Procession of the Catholic League on the Île de la Cité in 1593*.

Life in Paris under Louis XIII and Louis XIV is illustrated in the first thirteen rooms on the first floor: the city underwent rapid transformation and enrichment, as we see in Rooms 19 and 20, the *Grand Cabinet* and the *Grand Chamber* from the Hôtel de la Rivière in Place des Vosges, in which the architect Le Vau and the painter Le Brun worked.

The rooms that follow (of which certain were part of the apartment in which Madame de Sévigné lived for twenty years) are dedicated to the Paris of the 1600s and the 1700s through the end of the reign of Louis XV. The *Twenty Views of Paris* painted by Nicolas Raguenet, precious, basic documents for understanding of the urban development of Paris in this period, are outstanding (Room 29).

The first floor ends with two important sections: through Room 48, the Parisian home at the time of Louis XV (*boiseries* from the Hôtel de Broglie, the Hôtel Brulart de Genlis, the Hôtel de l'Aubespine, and others, and furniture and decorations in Rocaille style); through Room 64, Paris and the Parisian home until the

A view of an interior in the hôtel, and a beautiful gilded herm.

Jean Béraud, La Soirée *(ca. 1800).*

reign of Louis XVI (*The Fire at the Opera of the Royal Palace*, the *Bridge of Neuilly* by Hubert Robert, and, above all, in Room 58, the *Salon* that the engraver Demarteau commissioned of Boucher and Fragonard in 1765).

The collections referred to the period of the Revolution and the last two centuries are all grouped on the three floors of the Hôtel Le Peletier de Saint-Fargeau.

The 12 rooms of the second floor contain the richest and most important collections of Revolutionary material in all of France.

Among the museum's most interesting relics are the *bill of indictment of Louis XVI* and the *key of the Temple* (in which the royal family was imprisoned), the *dressing table and chair* used by Marie-Antoinette in the Tower of the Temple (on the table are perfume bottles and a miniature of the Dauphin which the queen made during her imprisonment), the *shaving plate and razors* of the king, a *game of tombola* and an *exercise book* belonging to the Dauphin, a *model of the guillotine*, and the *page of the appeal* which Robespierre was signing when he was arrested (the first two letters of his surname and his bloodstains can still be seen).

Our visit continues in Rooms 115 to 125 on the ground floor, with the Paris of the First Empire (*Portrait of Madame Récamier* by F. Gérard) through the revolution of 1848, with *portraits of protagonists of the times*.

There follow, on the first floor in Rooms 126 through 147, illustrations of the city from the Second Empire down to our times. One of the most outstanding exhibits is the extraordinary decoration of the Fouquet jewellery shop, done by Alphonse Mucha in 1900 for the new shop that the jeweller had opened in no. 6 Rue Royale. Also of note is the decorative scheme of the ballroom conceived in 1925 by the Catalan painter José-Lluis Sert for the Parisian *hôtel* of the de Wendel family.

PLACE DES VOSGES

Perfectly square, 108 metres on each side, the square is completely surrounded by 36 old and picturesque mansions, with porticoes on the ground floor surmounted by two orders of windows. In the centre of the square, among its trees and flower

One of the entrances to the 17th-century Place des Vosges.

Place des Vosges, the heart of the Marais.

beds, is the *marble statue of Louis XIII on horseback,* a copy of the original by P. Biard destroyed during the Revolution. The square stands on the site of the Hôtel des Tournelles, where Henri II died in a joust in 1559. The square was designed by Henri IV in 1607 and completed in 1612. In the middle of the southern side is the splendid **Pavilion of the King,** built for Henri IV himself, and opposite it is the Pavilion of the Queen. At no. 1-B Madame de Sévigné was born, at no. 21 Richelieu lived, at no. 6, the former **Hôtel de Rohan-Guéménée,** Victor Hugo lived from 1832 to 1848. Today this building contains the **Victor Hugo Museum,** in which are souvenirs and objects recalling the most important aspects of his life, besides 350 drawings which bear witness to his great and versatile genius.

RUE ST-ANTOINE – This is the continuation of Rue de Rivoli going as far as Place de la Bastille. Enlarged in the 14th century, it became a meeting place and fashionable promenade. Here, in 1559, Henri II organised a joust to celebrate the marriage of his daughter, but he was wounded in the eye by the lance of the captain of his Scots Guards, Montgomery, and he died soon after being taken to the Hôtel des Tournelles.

ST-PAUL - ST-LOUIS – This is another fine example of the Jesuit-style church, the oldest in this style after that of the Carmelite monastery. It was built between 1627 and 1641 and took its

Baroque inspiration from the Church of Gesù in Rome. The façade, with its superimposed orders of columns, is so high that it hides the dome, a phenomenon rarely found elsewhere since in later buildings (Dôme-des-Invalides, Sorbonne, Val-de-Grâce) the dome can clearly be seen. The **interior** is well lit, without aisles but with linking chapels. Over the crossing is the fine cupola, on top of which is a lantern. The church contained many works of art, but these suffered great losses during the Revolution, when the reliquaries containing the hearts of Louis XIII and Louis XIV

The façade of the church of St-Paul-St-Louis.

The Hôtel de Béthune-Sully, with its elegant façade.

were melted down. In the transept are three 17th century panels, depicting *Scenes from the Life of St Louis.* The fourth, which has been lost, is substituted by one by Delacroix (1827) representing *Christ in the Garden of Olives.* A marble statue by Germain Pilon (16th century) of *Our Lady of Sorrows* stands in the chapel on the left of the chancel.

Also in Rue St-Antoine, at no. 62, is the **Hôtel de Béthune-Sully.** Built in 1624 by Du Cerceau, it was bought in 1634 by Béthune-Sully, former minister of Henri IV. Part of it today is the seat of the Historical Monuments Department. The **court of honor** is one of the finest examples of the Louis XIII style: the pediments are decorated and the dormer windows carved and enriched by a series of statues representing the *Elements* and the *Seasons.* A garden links the building with Place des Vosges.

PLACE DE LA BASTILLE

Rue St-Antoine ends here, in this square famous for its memories of the Revolution. Here stood the massive fortress built under Charles V between 1370 and 1382. It later became a State prison: among its inmates were Cagliostro, Fouquet, and the mysterious figure who became known as the 'Man in the Iron Mask'. The ill-famed prison was thus the first and most important objective of the popular uprising which broke out on 14 July 1789, when thousands of enraged Parisians marched against what was considered the symbol of the monarchy's despotism. The Bastille, held by its governor De Launay with only 32 Swiss guards and 82 invalids, soon fell into the people's hands; the governor was put to death and the prisoners (only seven) freed. The next day the demolition of the prison began, lasting until the following year. When the demolition was completed, the people danced on what had been the foundations of the terrible Bastille. Today, lines on the paving stones of the square mark the outlines of the former fortress. In the centre of the square is the **July Column,** built between 1831 and 1840 in memory of the Parisians killed in July 1830. Their bodies, together with those of the victims of February 1848, are enclosed in the marble base; their names are engraved on the shaft of the column. At the top of the 52-metre high column (which can be climbed via a stairway with 238 steps) is the *figure of Liberty* and a platform commanding a splendid view of the Marais quarter, the Île de la Cité and the Ste-Geneviève Hill.

OPÉRA-BASTILLE - The Opéra-Bastille was inaugurated on 14 July 1989, the anniversary of the fall of the prison, as part of the celebrations for the Bicentennial of the French Revolution. It was designed by Carlos Ott: its façade is a curved expanse of glass behind which is the main auditorium, with a capacity of 2,700 and a rotating stage.

ARSENAL LIBRARY- Standing at no. 1 Rue de Sully, the building was constructed by Sully in 1594, while the reconstruction of the façade was done by Philibert Delorme. The library was created in 1757 by the War Minister, Marquis Paulmy d'Argenson, and later enriched by the Count d'Artois, the future Charles X. Today it contains more than one and one-half million volumes, 120,000 prints, 15,000 manuscripts, many illuminated manuscripts, and important documents concerning the history of the theatre. Its rooms are decorated with fine paintings from the 18th century. An interesting visit is that to the apartment of Charles Nodier, who was librarian from 1824 to 1844.

HÔTEL DE SENS - Situated at no. 1 Rue du Figuier, this is the only other example in Paris, after the Hôtel de Cluny, of the great medieval private mansions. It was built between 1475 and 1507 as the residence of the archbishops of Sens (of which Paris was a dependence until 1622). It was considerably restored in 1911, when it became the property of the city of Paris.
The façade is embellished at the corners by cylindrical turrets and has Guelph windows and dormer windows with Flamboyant Gothic decoration. Through the entrance with its pointed arch, one enters the courtyard, with its square tower containing a staircase. In the Hôtel de Sens is the **Forney Library,** containing documents of a technical and scientific nature and collections of posters.

The Hôtel de Sens and the July Column at the center of Place de la Bastille; in the background, the modern Opéra-Bastille building.

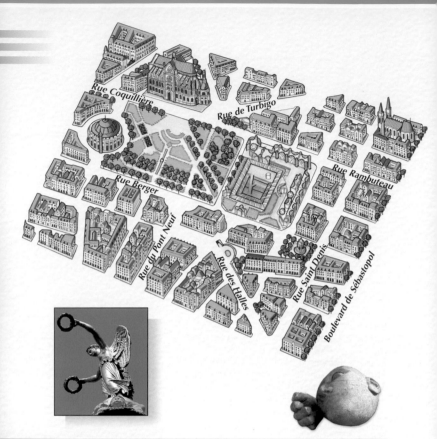

9th Itinerary

Beaubourg
and Les Halles

PLACE DU CHÂTELET - The square takes its name from the ancient fortress, the Grand Châtelet, built to defend the Pont au Change in front of it and destroyed under Napoleon I. But the present appearance of the square dates from the time of Napoleon III. In the centre is the **Châtelet Fountain** (also called the Fountain of Victory or 'of the Palm'), with its base adorned by sphinxes and statues, dating from 1858. The column was erected in 1808 to celebrate the victories of Napoleon I. On either side of the square are two theatres, both designed by Davioud. On the right (standing with one's back to the Seine) is the **Théâtre de la Ville** and on the left the **Théâtre du Châtelet,** which with seating for 3,600 has the largest auditorium in Paris.

Decorative elements in Place du Châtelet; the fountain as it appears today and as it was painted in the 1800s by Étienne Bouhot.

ST-JACQUES TOWER – Dominating the whole square, the tower is all that is left of the old Church of St-Jacques-la-Boucherie, destroyed in 1797. Erected between 1508 and 1522, it is 52 metres high and its style is purest Flamboyant Gothic. It has narrow windows alternating with niches surmounted by spires and pinnacles, within which are many statues. The statue on the top of the tower represents *St James the Greater* (Chenillon, 1870). A statue of *Pascal* stands at the base of the tower, under the vaults, in memory of the experiments on the weight of air which he made in 1648. The tower today contains a weather station.

ST-MERRI – Entrance to the Church of St-Merri, or St Medericus, who died here in the 7th century, is at no. 76 Rue de la Verrerie. The church, begun in 1520 and completed in 1612, is strangely enough in the earlier Flamboyant Gothic style. The **façade** underwent various works of remodelling in the 17th and 18th centuries and today has a portal adorned with modern statues; alongside the church is the 17th-century bell tower.

Like the façade, the **interior**, with four aisles, was remodelled at various times: under Louis XV, the architect Boffrand and the Slodtz brothers demolished the *jubé*, transformed the pointed arches into round arches, and covered the pillars of the chancel with gilded stuccoes and marble. The fine 16th-century stained glass in the transept and chancel and the ribbed vault over the transept crossing remain. The church also contains some fine works of art: a 17th-century organ, a *Virgin and Child* by Van Loo, and wood inlays by the Slodtz brothers in the chancel and sacristy.

FOUNTAIN OF THE INNOCENTS – This is one of the masterpieces of French Renaissance. Designed by Pierre Lescot and sculpted by Jean Goujon, it is the oldest fountain in Paris, erected between 1547 and 1550 as a square structure, with Classical arcades on each side and many bas-reliefs of nymphs, marine gods, tritons, and Victories. The fountain originally stood at the corner of Rue St-Denis and the present Rue

The St-Jacques Tower and the Church of St-Merri.

The Fountain of the Innocents as it appears today.

Berger, where it was against a wall so that only three sides were visible. The fourth side was sculpted by Pajou and added in 1788, when the fountain was moved to where it still stands today.

BOURSE DE COMMERCE –
The ancient grain market built in 1765 by the provost of the merchants is today the Stock Exchange, a striking circular

A view of the Bourse de Commerce and the sculpture entitled L'Écoute, by Henri de Miller.

building set off by a monumental order of paired pilaster strips. The offices form a crown around the huge centre hall, which is surmounted by a glass-and-steel dome.

Reorganization of the area between the Bourse building and the Church of Saint-Eustache has included construction of ultramodern structures and public spaces embellished with works of contemporary art, like *L'Écoute* by Henri de Miller: a colossal head that seems to cock its ear to what is happening around it.

FORUM DES HALLES

Les Halles, the oldest district of Paris, is also the liveliest and most vivacious. Émile Zola once described it, with a colourful expression, as the 'belly of Paris'. In fact, the city wholesale grocery market once stood here: ten pavilions of iron, steel, and cast iron. When the market was transferred to Rungis in March 1969, the district seemed suddenly to have lost all of its vivacity as well as its main purpose. It needed new life: and so began the biggest transformation work ever carried out in the heart of a city. Within this new concept of urban space, in the place where the city used to go to feed itself, there now rose a new form of culture and commerce: the Forum, over forty thousand square metres of glass and aluminum, marble stairways, and furniture, developed over four underground levels and around a quadrangular open-air square. In the Forum, inaugurated on 4 September 1979

Old and new: Les Halles in the 19th century and with today's glass-and-aluminum Forum structures.

and based on a project by two architects, Claude Vasconi and Georges Pencreac'h, we find boutiques selling clothing and objets d'art, grocers' shops and other shops selling household items, entertainment halls, restaurants, movie-houses, banks, and information centres.

Almost the entire commercial centre area faces onto covered galleries of large windows, so that the daylight penetrates to all the levels. There is also an underground station linked to four lines of the Métro and two lines of the RER.

BEAUBOURG (Centre Georges Pompidou)

For nearly all visitors and tourists, the 'Georges Pompidou National Centre of Art and Culture' is today simply 'Beaubourg'. Situated between Rue Rambuteau and Rue St-Merri and between Rue St-Martin and Rue Renard, the Beaubourg, with its audacious architecture, is now a part of our culture and civilization. In 1969, the then President of the Republic, Georges Pompidou, decided to create an important cultural centre in the area known as the 'plateau Beaubourg'. An international call to tender was announced and 49 countries participated with 681 projects: the project of Renzo Piano and Richard Rogers was accepted. Building began in April 1972 and the centre was opened by Giscard d'Estaing on the 31 January 1977. The building, an 'urban machine' as it has often been described, occupies an area of one hundred thousand square metres. With a revolutionary idea, all the structures normally placed inside a building, such as escalators, lifts, safety exits, and vertical ducts here have been situated on the outside. This idea of the general evolution of spaces is continued on the inside: every expression of contemporary art is a part of our lives and should be accessible to everyone at any time. The Beaubourg is not intended to be a museum of works of art but instead a place for meeting and exchanging ideas between artists and the public, the public and the things, where everyone can freely move around and approach the principal expressions of contemporary art and culture. Some curious pieces of information: the Beaubourg is

higher and longer than the Parthenon of the Athens Acropolis (it is in fact 42 metres high and 166 metres long); it weighs 15,000 tons of steel compared with the 7,000 tons of iron in the Eiffel Tower; each type of external pipeline is painted a different colour because each colour corresponds to a different function: blue corresponds to the climate-control plant, yellow the electrical installation, red the circulation, and green the water circuits.

A detail of the modern architecture of the Beaubourg.

The exterior of the Centre Georges Pompidou.

The building underwent extensive interior restoration work lasting more than two years, during which time the spaces were reorganized, the works redistributed, and the museum tour replanned.

As part of this work, the **Public Information Library** was given the northern portion of the first level, all the second, and a part of the third: here, anyone can consult, free of charge, the 350,000 printed documents via the 370 multimedia workstations.

The sixth level is given over to a restaurant and various temporary exhibits, while the fourth and fifth levels are occupied by the great **National Museum of Modern Art**.

NATIONAL MUSEUM OF MODERN ART – The museum extends over more than 14,000 square meters and can host 1,400 works on permanent exhibit.

On the fourth floor, which opens with a large canvas by Jean Tinguely, are exhibited works of contemporary art; that is, dated from 1960 to the present.

The contemporary collections begin with American Pop Art of the 1960s (works by Andy Warhol, Claus Oldenberg, Roy Lichtenstein) and with New Realism (Raymond Hains, Tinguely, Niki de Saint-Phalle). There follow all the other artistic currents of the second half of the 20th century: kinetic art (Vasarely, Soto), poor art, conceptual art, the Cobra movement, hyper-realism, new trends in figurative painting. On the fifth floor are displayed the 900 works that cover the period between 1900 and the Sixties: the Fauves (Derain, Vlaminck, Dufy, Matisse), the German painters of the 'Die Brücke' movement, Cubism (Picasso, Braque, Morandi, Gris), the Dada movement, Surrealism, and Abstract Art.

On the completely remodelled Beaubourg terraces, Renzo Piano has created pools of water that reflect the statues of Laurens, Calder, and Mirò placed nearby.

Besides the Museum of Modern Art and the Public Library, the Pompidou Centre also contains two other departments: Cultural Development (with live shows, cinema, and audio-visual presentations) and the famous IRCAM (Acoustic-Musical Research and Coordination Institute), located below the Igor Stravinsky fountain and organized by the composer Hector Berlioz to develop the techniques required for renewal of modern musical composition.

PLACE IGOR STRAVINSKY – Between Place Georges Pompidou and Rue du Cloître-St-Merri, there opens Place Igor Stravinsky, a space almost totally occupied by an original, brightly-coloured, and amusing fountain by Jean Tinguely, the kinetic sculptor of the Nouveau Réalisme group, and Niki de Saint-Phalle.

QUARTIER DE L'HORLOGE - To one side of the Pompidou Centre is the modern pedestrian quarter of l'Horloge, which owes

its name and its fame to the celebrated clock by Jacques Monestier, installed in 1979. Built of brass and steel, the mechanism is electronically driven and programmed.
At the stroke of each hour, a figure armed with shield and sword fights and defeats the three animals by which it is surrounded and that symbolize three elements: Dragon-Earth, Bird-Air, Crab-Water.

ST-EUSTACHE

The entertaining fountain in Place Igor Stravinsky and, below, the great clock known as the 'Defender of Time'.

Considered the most beautiful church in Paris after Notre-Dame, St-Eustache stands at the edge of Les Halles. Its construction continued over a long period of time: in 1532 the foundation stone was laid, but only in 1637 could the church be said to be complete. Designed by Lemercier, it combines in an original way a Gothic structure with Renaissance decoration. The passage from one style to the other can be followed best of all in the sides and in the apse, which have three orders of windows, tall pilasters, and great flying arches, while the rose windows are typical of the Renaissance.

Interior. Its dimensions are imposing: almost 100 metres long, 44 metres wide, and 33 metres high. It has double aisles around the nave, with transept and chancel. The round Renaissance arcades in the nave are divided by bundle pillars, while the vaulting of the nave, chancel, and transept is in the Flamboyant Gothic style. A great organ, made in 1844, stands above the entrance, and important concerts are still given in the church: In a chapel in the chancel is the *tomb of Colbert,* the famous Minister of Finance under Louis XIV: the sepulchre was designed by Le Brun; Coysevox sculpted the statues of *Colbert* and *Abundance* and Tuby that of *Fidelity.* Works by Rubens, Luca Giordano, and the Sienese Manetti can be found in other chapels.

The apse of the church of St-Eustache, with the Lady Chapel.

RUE DE TURBIGO – This street leads from the Les Halles quarter to Place de la République. Nearby, after Rue Étienne Marcel, is the **Tour de Jean-sans-Peur,** today incorporated in a school building (at no. 20 Rue de Turbigo). Square in form and crowned with overhanging battlements (from which boiling oil used to be poured), the tower was erected in 1408 by Jean-sans-Peur (John the Fearless) following the assassination of the Duke of Orléans ordered by him.

RUE ST-DENIS – Built in the 7th century, Rue St-Denis soon became the most wealthy street in Paris. Along it the kings moved in solemn procession when they entered Paris to go to Notre-Dame; this was also the street along which the dead were taken to be buried at St-Denis.

ST-LEU - ST-GILLES – The church, at no. 92 Rue St-Denis, is dedicated to two saints of the 6th century, St Lupus, the bishop of Sens, and St Giles, a hermit from Provence. Its construction goes back to 1320, but it has been much restored and remodelled. Two towers with cusps stand at the sides of the façade; the bell tower on the left was added in 1858.
In the **interior**, the vaults in the nave are in the Gothic style, while the chancel is Classical and higher than the nave. It has some fine works of art, including the keystones of the vaults, a 16th-century marble group representing the *Virgin and St Anne,* and some alabaster bas-reliefs, brought here from the former Cemetery of the Innocents, at the entrance to the sacristy.

ST-NICOLAS-DES-CHAMPS – Standing in Rue St-Martin, another of the streets which cross Rue Turbigo, this is dedicated to St Nicholas, a 4th-century bishop from Asia Minor. It was built in the 12th century, reconstructed in the 15th century, and further enlarged in following centuries. The façade and bell tower, fine examples of the Flamboyant Gothic style, have been restored.

On the right-hand side, there is a splendid Renaissance **portal** (1581), the graceful forms of which may be a copy of one of the doors of the Hôtel des Tournelles. The apse too, with its large windows, is an imposing Renaissance structure.

After leaving the church, in Rue Volta no. 3, we find the **oldest house in Paris**, dating back as far as the 13th or 14th century.

CONSERVATOIRE NATIONAL DES ARTS ET MÉTIERS – At no. 292 Rue St-Martin, this was once the site of the Abbey of St-Martin-des-Champs, built in 1061 and reconstructed in the 13th century. The Conservatory of Arts and Professions, created in 1794, took over this site in 1799; today it includes a school and museum. Of the former abbey, only the refectory and chancel remain today. Through the entrance one reaches the main court-yard, on the right of which is the **refectory** of the old monastery, now used as a library. This 13th-century refectory is a master-piece by Pierre de Montreuil. Measuring 43 by 12 metres and gracefully divided down the centre by seven slender columns, the hall has the purest of Gothic lines. Its tall mullioned windows, Gothic vaulting, and perfect proportions make it a splendid work. Halfway along the right side is a door, on the outside of which are fine carvings.

From the Court of Honour, a staircase leads up to the **Musée des Arts et Métiers**, where original machines (or models) document the lengthy progress of technology and industry. The permanent collections are arranged by themes in exhibits on three floors; seven departments illustrate the full story of scientific progress: scientific instruments, materials, construction, communications, energy, machines, and transport.

SQUARE DU TEMPLE – On this site there once stood a vast com-plex of buildings occupied by the religious and military order of the Knights Templar. Founded in 1118 in the Holy Land, the order was established in Paris in 1140 and grew swiftly. The Knights Templar were independent of the Crown and came to own the entire Marais quarter, forming a powerful financial group which soon constituted a real state within the state. On 13 October 1307, Philippe le Bel had all the Knights Templar in France imprisoned, and in 1314 had their Grand Master Jacques de Molay and his followers burnt at the stake. The order was thus suppressed, and the Templar buildings passed into the hands of the Hospitaliers de St-Jean-de-Jérusalem, or the Knights of St John of Jerusalem, the original name of the Knights of Malta.

This order too was suppressed by the Revolution, and the Temple became the prison of the royal family. On 13 August 1792, Louis XVI, Marie-Antoinette, their two children, and the king's sister were closed in the Temple Tower, 45 metres high with walls 3 metres thick.

After the execution of the royal family, in order to avoid the site attracting Royalist pilgrimages, it was decided in 1808 to demol-ish the Tower. The whole area was gradually transformed into an open-air market, particularly of old clothes, known as the **Carreau du Temple.** In 1857, the square was remodelled by Haussmann as it stands today, including the covered market.

PLACE DE LA RÉPUBLIQUE – Laid out by Haussmann in 1854, the square is now a vast bottleneck of traffic. In the centre is the

monument to the Republic, erected by Morice in 1883. On the base are large bronze bas-reliefs by Dalou, representing the great events in the history of the Republic.

PLACE DE LA NATION – Formerly called Place du Trône, because of the great throne erected here on 26 August 1660 for Louis XIV and his young wife, Maria-Theresa, on their entrance into Paris. During the Revolution, the throne was torn down and the guillotine erected in its place: the square was thus renamed Place du Trône-Renversé (Square of the Overturned Throne). It was given its present name in 1880, when France's national day, the 14th of July, was first celebrated here. In the centre of the square, surrounded by flower beds, is a basin with the *bronze group of the Triumph of the Republic,* sculpted by Dalous for Place de la République but erected here in 1899. At the sides of Avenue du Trône, which begins here, are the two columns erected by Ledoux and surmounted by the *statues of Philippe II Auguste and St Louis.* This avenue becomes Cours de Vincennes and leads directly to Vincennes, the large residential suburb, with its splendid park and magnificent castle.

PÈRE-LACHAISE CEMETERY

This is the largest and most important cemetery in Paris, because of the many tombs of illustrious men within its tranquil walls. A visit to the tombs becomes almost a historical pilgrimage through the realms of painting, poetry, and philosophy. There are the tombs of the writers *de Musset, Molière, La Fontaine, Alphonse Daudet, the Hugo family, Beaumarchais, Paul Eluard, Oscar Wilde, Marcel Proust, Guillaume Apollinaire,* and *Balzac;* the composers *Chopin* (his heart is in Warsaw), *Bizet, Dukas,* and *Cherubini;* the painters *Géricault, David, Corot, Modigliani, Delacroix, De Nittis, Ingres, Daumier,* and *Seurat;* the philosophers and scientists *F. Arago, Auguste Comte, Gay-Lussac, Allan Kardec* (founder of the philosophy of the spirit), and *Peter Abelard* and his wife *Heloise;* the political and military leaders *Masséna, Ney, Blanqui, Lecomte, Murat,* and *Caroline Bonaparte;* the singer *Edith Piaf* and the Italian soprano *Adelina Patti,* the dancer *Isadora Duncan,* the actress *Sarah Bernhardt,* and *Jim Morrison,* lead singer of the mythical rock group *The Doors.*

At the centre of Place de la République stands the monument dedicated to the French Republic.

10th Itinerary

THE GREAT BOULEVARDS

These famous avenues extend for more than four kilometers in a wide sweep from Place de la Bastille to the Madeleine. As they now are, they were laid out last century by Haussmann. The boulevards had originally replaced Charles V's old city walls, stretching from the Bastille to the Gate of St-Denis, and the ramparts of Charles IX and Louis XIII, which went from the St-Denis Gate to the Madeleine and were demolished in the late 17th century. The boulevards were much frequented throughout the 19th century and through the early years of the 20th, when fashionable crowds filled the luxurious cafés, shops, and theatres which lined these wide streets. Today their fashionable character has been transformed into a more noisy and popular atmosphere.

135

BOULEVARD ST-MARTIN – This boulevard goes from Place de la République to the St-Martin Gate. It contains many cinemas and theatres, including the **Théâtre de la Renaissance** (1872) and alongside the **Théâtre de la Porte St-Martin,** built in 1781. The latter has remained famous because of the triumphant performances there by the great Sarah Bernhardt and by Coquelin, in the role of Cyrano (1897).

Porte St-Martin, on the boulevard of the same name; below, a detail of the decoration of the arch.

PORTE ST-MARTIN – This triumphal arch, 17 metres high, was erected by Bullet in 1674 to commemorate the taking of Besançon and the defeat of the Spanish, Dutch, and German armies. It has three vaults, and is covered with bas-reliefs carved by Le Hongre, Desjardins, Legros, and Marsy, representing on one side the *Capture of Besançon* and the *Breaking of the Triple Alliance* and on the other the *Capture of Limbourg* and the *Defeat of the Germans.*

PORTE ST-DENIS – This gate too, like the Porte St-Martin, has the form of a triumphal arch, with a single vault measuring 24 metres both in height and in width. Designed by Blondel and erected in 1672, it has sculpture by the Anguier brothers and was intended to celebrate the victories of Louis XIV in Germany, when in less than two months the French king succeeded in conquering forty strongholds. The allegorical bas-reliefs representing *Holland* and the *Rhine* are fine works.

After the Porte St-Denis, the boulevard takes the name of **Boulevard de Bonne-Nouvelle.** A stairway on the right leads up to the **Church of Notre-Dame-de-Bonne-Nouvelle,** its bell tower being all that remains of the church rebuilt under Anne of Austria. Inside, apart from a fine *statue of the Virgin* (17th century), are two original 18th-century panels attributed to Mignard: *Henrietta of England with her Three Children before St Francis of Sales* and *Anne of Austria and Henrietta of England.*

After **Boulevard Poissonnière,** we reach **Boulevard Montmartre,** one of Paris' busiest streets, running from Rue Montmartre to Boulevard des Italiens. At no. 10 is the **Grévin Museum,** founded in 1882 by the caricaturist Grévin and containing all sorts of magic devices and amusements, including waxworks of great figures and famous scenes in history. Near the museum, at no. 7, is the **Théâtre des Variétés,** home of vaudeville and light opera, in which many works by composers such as Offenbach, Tristan Bernard, and Sacha Guitry were performed.

BOULEVARD DES ITALIENS – This boulevard's period of maximum splendour began during the time of the Directory and continued until the end of the Second Empire. Great financiers, famous journalists and distinguished men of letters frequented its cafés, the *Café Anglais*, the *Café Tortoni*, and the *Café Riche* (the latter unfortunately has disappeared: in its place, at no. 16, is the Banque Nationale de Paris).

OPÉRA-COMIQUE – Standing at the end of the boulevard in Place Boieldieu, it was rebuilt by Bernier in 1898 after two fires. The comic operas from Italian repertory were performed here in the past - works by such composers as Mascagni, Rossini, and Leoncavallo.

RUE LAFAYETTE – This street leads off Boulevard Haussmann, and on the corner are *Les Galeries Lafayette*, one of the largest department stores in the city. The crossroads where it meets Rue Le Peletier was the scene of Felice Orsini's attempt on the life of Napoleon III on 14 January 1858.

BOULEVARD HAUSSMANN – The boulevard is named after the man who was largely responsible for replanning the city of Paris, Baron G. E. Haussmann, Prefect of the Seine from 1853 to 1870. The wide avenue, begun in 1857, was completed in 1926. At no. 26 is the house where Marcel Proust lived from 1906 to 1919.

CHAPELLE EXPIATOIRE – The Expiatory Chapel is in the Square Louis XVI, surrounded by a green and tranquil garden. Here there was a small cemetery, dating from 1722, in which were buried the Swiss Guards who fell on 10 August 1792 at the Tuileries and the victims of the guillotine, a total of 1343 persons, including Louis XVI and Marie-Antoinette, whose bodies were later transferred, on 21 January 1815, to St-Denis. Louis XVIII had Fontaine build this chapel between 1815 and

The interior of the dome of Les Galeries Lafayette, supported by ten metal pillars.

The exterior of the chapel in which, as tradition has it, the bodies of Louis XVI and Marie-Antoinette were brought following their executions.

1826. In front of it is a cloister and a small garden, and on the right the *tombs of Charlotte Corday* and *Philippe-Égalité*. Inside the chapel are two marble groups, one by Bosio (1326) of *Louis XVI*, and another by Cortot (1836) of *Marie-Antoinette Sustained by Religion*, portrayed with the features of the king's sister Elisabeth.

PLACE ST-AUGUSTIN – The square is at the point where Boulevard Haussmann and Boulevard Malesherbes meet. It is dominated by the imposing mass of the **Church of St-Augustin,** built by Baltard between 1860 and 1871 in a curious mixture of Byzantine and Renaissance styles, using metal girders for the first time in a church. It was here that in 1886 Charles-Eugène de Foucauld formalised his conversion.

JACQUEMART-ANDRÉ MUSEUM – The museum is in an elegant late 19th-century building at no. 158 Boulevard Haussmann, which the owner, Mme Nélie Jacquemart-André, left to the Institut de France in 1912. It contains large collections of 18th-century European and Italian Renaissance works. On the ground floor are paintings and drawings by Boucher, Chardin, and Watteau and sculptures, by Houdon and by Pigalle, recalling the era of Louis XV, while the 17th and 18th centuries are well represented by Canaletto, Murillo, Rembrandt, and others. The Italian works include paintings by Botticelli, terracottas by the Del-

Two typically Parisian urban accoutrements: the so-called 'Morris column', a circular 'billboard' with a bulbous domed top, used for posting theatre posters and advertisements, and a Métro station sign by Hector Guimard.

la Robbia family, sculpture by Donatello, and large canvases by Tintoretto and Paolo Uccello.

CATHEDRAL OF ST-ALEXANDRE-NEVSKY – This is the Russian Orthodox church of Paris. At no. 12 Rue Daru, it was built in 1860 in the Neo-Byzantine style of Moscow's churches. The interior is embellished with gilded stuccoes, icons, and frescoes.

PARC MONCEAU – This splendid garden, its main entrance on Boulevard de Courcelles, is the centre of a fashionable part of the city. The park was laid out by the painter Carmontelle for the Duke of Orléans in 1778. On 22 October 1797, the first parachutist in the world, Garnerin, landed in the park. In 1852, the financier Péreire had two splendid mansions built here, and later the engineer Alphand opened up part of it as an English-style public garden, with ruins, small temples, a tiny lake, and imitation rocks. At the entrance is the **Pavilion de Chartres**, a rotunda with columns designed by Ledoux. The oval **Naumachia** basin is surrounded by a colonnade, brought from the mausoleum of Henri II at St-Denis, which was never completed. Nearby is a Renaissance-style arcade, originally part of the Hôtel de Ville.

CERNUSCHI MUSEUM – With its entrance at no. 7 Avenue Velasquez, this was the residence of the banker Cernuschi, who in 1896 left it in his will to the city of Paris, along with the works of Oriental art which he had collected. These include important Neolithic terracottas, bronzes, and jades. Worth seeing are a fine stone statue representing a *Seated Bodhisattva,* from the 5th century, and several precious works of ancient painting, including the *Horse and Grooms,* a masterpiece of 8th-century T'ang painting on silk.

NISSIM DE CAMONDO MUSEUM – This museum, at no. 63 Rue de Monceau, was the residence of the Count de Camondo, who left it and his collections of 18th-century art to the nation in 1936 in memory of his son Nissim, who had died in the war. The mansion is a magnificent and accurate example of a typically elegant dwelling in the era of Louis XVI. It contains pieces of furniture by the greatest cabinetmakers, clocks, silverware and splendid dinner services, and canvases by Guardi, Jongkind, Vigée-Lebrun, and others.

PLACE DE CLICHY – This busy square, always filled with people and traffic, was the scene of furious fighting in March 1814 between the Russian troops, who had entered Paris with the other Allies and had their bivouac in the Champs-Élysées, and Marshal Moncey, to whom the monument was later erected in the centre of the square. It also stands at the beginning of Boulevard de Clichy and Boulevard de Rochechouart, which runs around the base of the hill of Montmartre.

MONTMARTRE

Montmartre was and is one of the most picturesque and curious quarters of Paris. It stands on a limestone hill 130 metres high where, according to the legend, St Denis, the first bishop of Paris, was beheaded in about 250 AD along with the priests Eleutherius and Rusticus.
Because of its strategic position, dominating the whole of Paris, Montmartre has also had an important part in the city's political history. In fact the Commune began from an incident here in March 1871. Then, throughout the 19th century, Montmartre was the Mecca of all the Bohemian artists and for a long time it

The Moulin-Rouge at night. It was here that the cancan was invented.

maintained its place as the literary and artistic centre of the whole city.

MONTMARTRE CEMETERY – The entrance is in Avenue Rachel. Opened in 1795, it contains the tombs of many famous figures: painters like *Fragonard, Degas,* and *Chassériau,* writers such as *Théophile Gautier, Edmond* and *Jules de Goncourt, Stendhal, Émile Zola, Alexandre Dumas the Younger,* and *Heinrich Heine,* and the composers *Hector Berlioz* and *Offenbach.* There are also the tombs of the playwrights *Labiche* and *Giraudoux,* the actors *Sacha Guitry* and *Louis Jouvet,* the celebrated Russian ballet dancer *Nijinsky,* and the famous *Alphonsine Plessis,* better known as the 'Lady of the Camellias'.

PLACE BLANCHE – At the foot of the Montmartre hill, the 'White Square' owes its name to the chalk roads which once existed here. It is overlooked by the long sails of the **Moulin-Rouge,** the music hall founded in 1889; among the artists who performed on its stage were Jane Avril, Valentin le Désossé, and

La Goulue, and here the cancan, immortalised in the canvases of Toulouse-Lautrec, was born.

From here, by way of Boulevard de Clichy, lined by many modern cinemas and beer halls, one reaches **Place Pigalle,** a bustling scene, particularly at night when its night clubs turn on their many lights. **Boulevard de Rochechouart,** which begins here, is also filled with places of entertainment, including the dance hall the *Boule-Noire,* at no. 120, and the *Taverne Bavaroise* in front of it. At no. 84 was the famous

Chat-Noir cabaret, founded in 1881 and recalled so often in the songs of Aristide Bruant.

ST-JEAN-DE-MONTMARTRE – Facing Square Jehan-Rictus, this church, the first in Paris to be built with reinforced concrete, was completed in 1904 by de Baudot. It is known to the people of the area as St-Jean-des-Briques (St John of the Bricks) because of its brick exterior.

BATEAU-LAVOIR – Continuing by way of Rue Ravignan, we reach a small square, Place Émile-Goudeau. This was the site of the Bateau-Lavoir, a small wooden building, unfortunately destroyed by a fire in 1970, where modern painting and poetry were born in about 1900. In it Picasso, Braque, and Gris worked (it was here that Picasso painted the *Demoiselles d'Avignon*, which marked the birth of Cubism), and while they were revolutionising the traditional canons of painting, Max Jacob and Apollinaire were doing the same for poetry.

RUE LEPIC – It begins in Place Blanche and winds up towards the top of the hill. In autumn there is an antique car rally which follows the street's steep curves. At no. 54 Vincent Van Gogh lived with his brother Théo. Nearby is the celebrated **Moulin de la Galette,** the last of the city's 30 windmills, which inspired paintings by Renoir and Van Gogh.

SACRÉ-CŒUR

Standing majestically on the top of the Montmartre hill, it was begun in 1876 by national subscription and consecrated in 1919. The architects who designed it (among them Abadie and Magne) built it in a curious style, a mixture of Romanesque and Byzantine. The four small domes and the large central dome, standing on the high drum, are typically Oriental. On the back

The broad stairs leading up to the basilica of the Sacré-Cœur and one of the two equestrian statues that stand in front of its portico.

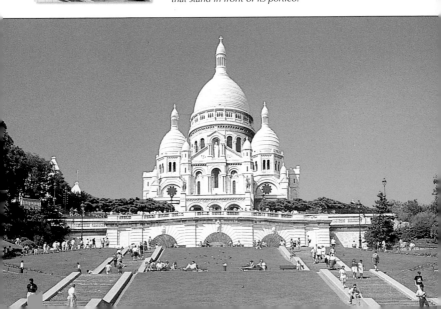

part, the square bell tower, 84 metres high, contains the **Savoyarde**, weighing 19 tons, one of the largest bells in the world. An imposing stairway leads up to the façade of the church, in front of which is a porch with three arches; above are the *equestrian statues of King Louis the Blessed* and *Joan of Arc*.

Interior. Its dimensions are impressive and the decorations of sculpture, paintings and mosaics are extremely elaborate. From inside the church, the visitor can descend to visit the crypt and can also climb up to the top of the dome, from which there is

The large mosaic in the chancel of the Sacré-Cœur, and an evocative nighttime view of the basilica.

a breathtaking panoramic view of Paris and the surrounding areas. To admire the white mass of Sacré-Cœur from a better vantage point, one should descend, either via the cable railway or down the ramps of steps, into Place St-Pierre below.

ST-PIERRE-DE-MONTMARTRE – This church is what is left of the abbey established by the Benedictine nuns at Montmartre. It was begun towards 1134 and completed by the end of the century. The façade was almost completely remodelled in the 18th century. In the **interior**, on the inside of the entrance wall, are four columns which came from a Roman temple which previously occupied the site. The church has three aisles divided by pillars, a transept and three apses. In the left aisle is the *tomb of Adélaide of Savoy*, wife of Louis VI 'le Gros', who founded the abbey.

PLACE DU TERTRE

This old square, once used as a meeting place and now lined with trees, is the heart of Montmartre, animated by warmth and colour. It is frequented by painters and a cosmopolitan crowd and comes alive particularly at night, when its cafés and night clubs fill with people and the small space in the centre of the square fills with artists, who work a little for themselves and a great deal for the tourists.

'AU LAPIN AGILE' – Walking down Rue Norvins, we come to the steep and picturesque Rue des Saules. In this area lived some of the most famous Parisian painters, among them Suzanne Valadon and Utrillo. On the corner of Rue St-Vincent, half hidden by an acacia tree, is the rustic cabaret 'Au Lapin Agile', which was originally called the 'Cabaret des Assassins' but which derived its present name ('At the Sign of the Agile Rabbit') from the sign painted by the artist Gill. Much frequented from 1908 to 1914 by penniless painters and poets who were soon to become celebrities, it is still today the scene of interesting literary gatherings.

Place du Tertre and its world of painters en plein air.

Towers in La Défense quarter; below, a view of the Grande Arche.

LA DÉFENSE

Urbanization of La Défense, conceived as a huge 130 hectare business area, commenced in 1955 in the area forming the extension of Neuilly bridge. Buildings are erected below a paved esplanade 120 metres long and 250 metres wide with steps down to the Seine and under which all highways pass. Of all the modern buildings characterized by pure, geometric shapes (the Fiat, Manhattan, Gan, and Elf-Aquitaine towers), the number one attraction is the CNIT (Centre National des Industries et Techniques) building that today hosts meeting halls, vast spaces for trade fairs and exhibits, a hotel, and many shops and restaurants). Built in coats of concrete by the architects Zehrfuss, Camelot, and Mailly, it has the audacious shape of an overturned shell resting on only three points of support.

THE 'GRANDE ARCHE' – Designed in 1982 by the Dane Johan Otto von Spreckelsen and inaugurated in July 1989, the Grande Arche consists of two towers, each 105 meters high, topped by a crosspiece. At the centre of the structure faced in Carrara marble and glass hangs a sort of large awning, the so-called 'Cloud'. Four elevators carry visitors to the evocative belvedere.

The New Architecture of Paris: La Défense and La Villette

LA VILLETTE

Since 13 March 1986, date of the last passage of Halley's comet, the La Villette park, with its 35 hectares extension, has been the seat of the **Cité des Sciences et de l'Industrie**.
Here we find the 'Géode', the largest cinema in the world, the 'Grand Halle', one of the loveliest architectural creations in metal of the 19th century, and the 'Zénith' theatre.
La Villette also contains the **Cité de la Musique**, with the recently-founded Musée de la Musique consecrated to the history of European music from the Renaissance to our times.

MUSÉE DE LA MUSIQUE - The itinerary through the museum is organized chronologically in nine sections, each of which presents a work of music representative of a period, complete with the score, the instrumental ensemble, and the setting. The works are *Orfeo* by Claudio Monteverdi, *Dardanus* by Jean-Philippe Rameau, Mozart's *Symphony No. 31 in D Major 'Paris'*, Berlioz's *Symphonie Fantastique*, *Robert le Diable* by Meyerbeer, Wagner's *Parsifal*, Saint Saëns' *Symphony No. 3*, *The Rite of Spring* by Igor Stravinsky, and *Ex-position* by Maurice Kagel.
The second part of the museum is dedicated to musical instruments and their crafting. Among the most important (and most beautiful) pieces on exhibit are the 17th-century Venetian lutes, the precious violins, including the Stradivarius that belonged to the celebrated Spanish virtuoso Sarasate, a Guarneri made by Andrea's nephew 'Giuseppe del Gesù', and a harp that belonged to the princess of Lamballe.
The 20th century is represented by, among other pieces, Frank Zappa's synthesizer.

The steel sphere at the Géode at La Villette.

BOIS DE BOULOGNE

Situated to the west of Paris, almost opposite the other park of Vincennes, the Bois de Boulogne, with its lawns, lakes, waterfalls and gardens, covers an area of 845 hectares. In the era of the Merovingian kings, it was a vast forest, called the Forêt du Rouvre, from the name of the oak-tree which grew abundantly there. In the 16th century, a church called Notre-Dame-de-Boulogne-sur-mer was erected, and gradually the name of Boulogne came to replace that of Rouvre. The place became a refuge for adventurers and bandits, so that in 1556 Henri II had it surrounded by a high wall with eight gates. It was replanned by Colbert and Louis XIV opened its gates to the public, with the result that the wood became a favourite place for promenades. Devastated in 1815 by the English and Russian armies when they camped there, the wood was given to the city in 1852 by Napoleon III, who commissioned Haussmann to replan and reorganise it: thus the wood became a vast park, inspired by London's Hyde Park, which the emperor had admired. Today the Bois de Boulogne includes lakes (**Lac Supérieur** and **Lac Inférieur),** waterfalls (the **Grande-Cascade),** parks (splendid the **Bagatelle,** with the mansions of the **Château** and the **Trianon**), museums (**Museum of Popular Arts and Traditions**), and famous sporting centres (the **Longchamp Hippodrome**, where the Gran Prix is run every year, and the **Auteuil Racecourse**).

VINCENNES

The castle was called the 'Versailles of the Middle Ages' and its history is closely linked to the history of France. The Forest of Vincennes was acquired by the crown in the 11th century and Philippe II Auguste had a manor house built there, to which Louis IX added the Chapelle. The castle, built by the Valois, was begun by Philippe VI in 1334 and completed by Charles V in 1370: in this period the **keep**, part of the Chapelle, and the surrounding walls were built. In 1654 Mazarin (who had become governor of Vincennes two years before) commissioned Le Vau to erect two symmetrical pavilions for the king and queen. From the beginning of the 16th century until 1734, the monarchs preferred Versailles to Vincennes, and the keep, where they had previously resided, became a state prison. In 1738 it became a porcelain factory (transferred to Sèvres in 1756) and Napoleon I converted it into a powerful arsenal, where in 1814 under its governor, General Daumensil, it opposed a heroic resistance to the Allies. It was modified by Louis-Philippe, who made it a rampart in the city's defences, and then its restoration was begun by Viollet-le-Duc under Napoleon III. Unfortunately, the castle was seriously damaged on 24 August 1944 when the Germans blew up part of its fortifications and set fire to the king's and queen's pavilions.

The **castle** is built in the form of a great rectangle, surrounded by a deep moat and formidable walls, on which there are towers which have been reduced in height. The entrance tower, the **Tour du Village,** is the only one apart from the keep which has not been lopped: it is 42 metres high and although the statues which adorned the outside of it have been lost, remains of Gothic decoration above the entrance portal can still be seen.

On the west side stands the magnificent **keep,** the sturdy but graceful lines of which convey the essential idea of 14th-century military art. The tower is 52 metres high and has four semicir-

Paris'Bois:
Boulogne and Vincennes

cular turrets at the corners. It too is surrounded by a wall and has its own moat; around the top of the wall runs a covered passage. In the centre of the side opposite the entrance, the south side, is a tower called the **Tour du Bois,** lowered by Le Vau and transformed into a monumental entrance. In the moat on the right, at the foot of the tower called the Tour de la Reine, is a column indicating the exact spot on which the Prince of Condé, Duke of Enghien, was executed on 20 March 1804, accused of plotting against Napoleon. The last side of the castle has five towers, all lowered in height.

Visiting the interior. The **Tour du Village** is the entryway to the huge courtyard, at the end of which on the left is the Chapelle.

THE CHAPELLE – Begun under Charles V in 1387, it was completed under Henri II in about 1522. In the Flamboyant Gothic style, it has stone rose windows and fine openwork on the façade. The spire has unfortunately been lost. The **interior** is without aisles and is illuminated by large windows, around the base of which runs a fine frieze. The stained glass, much restored, dates from the middle of the 16th century and depicts *Scenes from the Apocalypse.* In a chapel is the *tomb of the Duke of Enghien.*
In front of the chapel stands the **donjon**, which since 1934 has contained a historical museum. Its three floors thus have on display relics of the kings and of great figures who lived there. The floors are all laid out in the same way: they have a vast vaulted hall with a pillar in the centre and four small rooms in the corners, originally for private use but later converted into cells. From the terrace there is a splendid view of Paris, the wood, and the surrounding areas. Also in the courtyard are the two pavilions of the king and queen. In the first, on the right, Mazarin died in 1661; the second is now occupied by the Service Historique de la Marine.

BOIS DE VINCENNES – The Bois de Vincennes, 995 hectares in extension and the largest wood in Paris, was given to the city by Napoleon III to be transformed into a public park. This vast area includes, in the western part, the **Lac des Minimes,** a picturesque lake with three small islands, the nearby **Indochinese Temple,** erected in memory of the Vietnamese who died in World War I, the **Tropical Garden,** with its entrance at no. 45 Avenue de la Belle Gabrielle, and the **Floral Park,** in which hundreds of different types of flowers bloom all year round and which also contains the **Exotarium,** with tropical fish and reptiles.

ZOO – Its main entrance is in Avenue Daumesnil. It is one of the finest and largest zoos in Europe: it has an area of 17 hectares and contains 600 mammals and 700 birds. There is also a large artificial rock, 72 metres high, on which the mountain sheep are kept.

13th Itinerary

Louis XIV in a bust by Antoine Coysevox.

The castle of Versailles as rendered by J. H. Mansart in a painting from the first half of the 18th century.

A view of the Hall of Venus; in a niche on the right, the statue of Louis XIV by Jean Warin.

The center front of the palace, overlooking the Parterre d'Eau.

Versailles

HISTORY – Versailles at the time of Louis XIII was no more than a modest hunting lodge, situated about 20 kilometres south-west of Paris, built in 1624, and consisting of a square building with the present-day Marble Court in the centre. The creation of the great palace of Versailles was due to Louis XIV, who after the civil disturbances known as the Frondes decided to abandon Paris and transform his predecessor's simple hunting castle into a royal palace worthy of the splendid sovereign he wished to be. In 1668, Le Vau enlarged the original building to twice its size, giving it a wide façade on the side overlooking the park. The work of transforming the palace continued for a long time, under the direction of the other architects Hardouin-Mansart and Le Nôtre. The latter concentrated mainly on laying out the great gardens. On 6 October 1789, the royal family returned finally from Versailles to Paris in their gilded carriage, after a procession of market women had marched on the palace in an unprecedented demonstration. Without the royal court, the castle fell into a state of nearly total abandon, being sacked many times and robbed of many of its works of art, until in 1837 Louis-Philippe restored it and converted it into a museum of French history. Occupied by the Germans in 1870, it was the scene of the coronation of William of Prussia as emperor of Germany. In 1875, the Republic of France was proclaimed and in 1919 the peace treaty with Germany, putting an end to World War I, was signed there.

THE PALACE – Entering through the main gateway (which under Louis XIV was opened every morning at 5:30), we reach the first courtyard, called the **Ministers' Court,** at the end of which is the statue on horseback of Louis XIV (1835, by Cartellier and Petitot), with the two long buildings called the **Ministers' Wings** at the sides. Access to the second courtyard, the **Royal Court,** was permitted only to the carriages of the royal family: this has the **Gabriel Wing** or **Wing of Louis XV** on the right and the **Old Wing** on the left. Finally there is the third courtyard, the **Marble Court,** surrounded by the original building, the castle of Louis XIII, with its red bricks alternating with white stone. The three windows behind the balcony in the centre belonged to the king's bedroom: it was from here that on 1 September 1715, at 8:15 in the morning, the death of Louis XIV was announced; on the same balcony, 74 years later, Louis XVI appeared to placate the people who wanted him to return to Paris.

Through an arcade in the Royal Court we come upon the **west façade** of the palace, 580 meters long. It is the most famous and most beautiful, and overlooks the pleasant gardens. The central, projecting part was designed by Le Vau, while Hardouin-Mansart designed its two elegant wings. Each part consists of two orders, the lower of rusticated arcades and the upper of pillars, with pilaster strips and high windows. Above these again is a balustraded attic, in which were the apartments of the various members of the huge court, whereas the central part and two wings were where the family of the king and the royal princes lived.

The Mars Salon, used during soirées at court as a ballroom.

The War Salon, with the enormous stucco medallion by Coysevox of The Glory of Louis XIV.

A view of the resplendent Hall of Mirrors with its gilded wood chandeliers.

Interior. The interior is reached from the Royal Court by way of the Gabriel Wing. After the two vestibules comes the **Historical Museum,** with its eleven rooms illustrating the eras of Louis XIII and Louis XIV. At the end of the first gallery, via a stairway, is the entrance to the Opéra, designed by Gabriel in 1770 for the marriage of Louis XVI and Marie Antoinette: it is an oval-shaped chamber, with fine wood inlays and gilding on a blue background. Moving up to the first floor, particular attention should be given to the **Chapel Royal,** built to a design by Hardouin-Mansart between 1698 and 1710. It has three aisles, square pillars on which the arcades rest, and above them a gallery with fluted columns.

From the Chapel, we reach the **Hercules Salon**, vestibule of the **Great Apartment of the King,** consisting of six rooms richly decorated with stuccoes, polychrome marble and tapestries. Here the sovereign received the court three times a week, from six until ten

The Hall of Peace, which leads in to the Hall of Mirrors, and the lavishly-decorated Queen's Bedchamber.

o'clock in the evening. The rooms take their names from the various mythological subjects painted in the frescoes on the ceilings: thus the **Abundance Salon** is followed by the **Venus Salon** and by the **Diana Salon** (with a *bust* by Bernini depicting Louis XIV), which was the billiard room, the **Mars Salon**, used as a ballroom, with a magnificent Gobelins tapestry representing the *Entrance of Louis XIV into Dunkirk*, the **Mercury Salon**, once used for gaming and where the body of Louis XIV lay in state for eight days, and the **Hall of Apollo**, the music room, though during the day it became the throne room. Through the **War Salon**, with its cupola painted by Le Brun and with a fine stucco medallion by Coysevox depicting *Louis XIV on Horseback,* we reach the celebrated **Hall of Mirrors**. A masterpiece designed by Hardouin-Mansart and built between 1678 and 1684, it is 75 metres long and 10 wide, and its ceiling is decorated with paintings by Le Brun illustrating French victories. Seventeen large windows corresponding to the same number of windows on the wall opposite, look out onto the park; at the time of Louis XIV, the hall was illuminated in the evening by the light of 3000 candles. It was also embellished with tapestries, statues, and orange trees in silver vases. At the end of the Hall of Mirrors is the **Peace Salon**, so called because of the oval painting over the fireplace depicting *Louis XV Bringing Peace to Europe* (Lemoyne, 1729).

Next to the Hall is the **Suite of the King**. This consists of the **Council Chamber,** where Louis XIV used to work with his ministers, the **King's Bedchamber,** decorated with white wood and gold, where Louis XIV died, and the famous **Oeil-de-Bœuf Salon**, in which every morning and evening the court dignitaries attended when the king rose and went to bed. Splendid too is the **Private Suite of the King**, in the Louis XV style. Returning to the Peace Salon, we

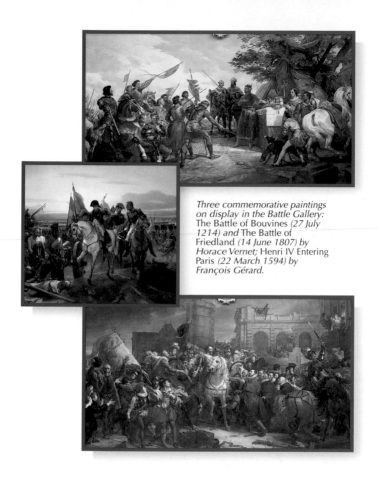

Three commemorative paintings on display in the Battle Gallery: The Battle of Bouvines (27 July 1214) and The Battle of Friedland (14 June 1807) by Horace Vernet; Henri IV Entering Paris (22 March 1594) by François Gérard.

pass on to the **Suite of the Queen**, built between 1671 and 1680. It consists of the **Queen's Bedchamber**, the **Room of the Nobles**, with the original furniture which was there in 1789, an **Antechamber**, with magnificent *Gobelins tapestries* and a *Portrait of Marie-Antoinette* by Vigée-Lebrun, and the **Queen's Guards' Room**, where on 6 October 1789 a group of insurgents from Paris killed several guards who were defending Marie-Antoinette. From this room one can visit the six small rooms in pure Louis XVI style which make up the so-called **Private Suite of the Queen.** Then, by the **Queen's Staircase**, designed by Hardouin-Mansart, we reach the **Great Guardroom**, in which there are two works by David, representing the *Coronation of Napoleon* and the *Distribution of the Eagles,* and one by Gros, representing *Murat at the Battle of Aboukir.* Nearby is the splendid **Battle Gallery**, built by Louis-Philippe in 1836: it takes its name from the paintings illustrating the most famous battles in France's history, among them the *Battle of Taillebourg* painted by Delacroix. Again by way of the Queen's Staircase, we go on to the rooms on the ground floor, decorated in Louis XIV style, with paintings from the reigns of Louis XV and Louis XVI.

A view of the palace against the
Parterre du Midi.

The Fountain of Latona in front of
the stairway leading up to the
castle.

THE GARDENS – These are considered the prototype of the
French-style garden because of their elegant style, full of artistic
and scenic inventions. The gardens were designed by Le Nôtre between 1661 and 1668 and occupy an area of 100 hectares. The
best panoramic view is without doubt from the terrace: at its ends
are the **Fountain of Diana** on the right and the **Point-du-Jour
Fountain** on the left, surrounded by bronze statues. On one side of
the terrace is the **Parterre du Nord** with basins and statues, among
them *Venus with the Tortoise* by Coysevox, a copy of the classical
Knife Grinder, and the so-called **Fountain of the Pyramid** by Girardon. Nearby, the **Basin of the Nymphs of Diana** and the **Allée
des Marmousets**, a double row of 22 basins adorned with bronze
putti from which the fountains spurt; this takes us as far as the
Basin of the Dragons and the **Basin of Neptune** (1740). On the
south side of the terrace is the box-edged **Parterre du Midi**. From
the balcony can be seen the **Orangerie,** which contained 3,000
trees (oranges, almonds, and pomegranates). Each year more than
150,000 types of flowers were planted there. Nearby are the great
Stairways of 100 Steps and the **Swiss Lake,** made between 1678
and 1682 by the Swiss Guards: at the end of it is *Bernini's statue of
Louis XIV,* which Girardon transformed into the statue of Marcus
Curtius. From the central terrace, we descend to the **Fountain of
Latona,** a masterpiece by Marsy depicting the goddess with her
children Diana and Apollo, dominating the concentric basins
which ascend in the form of a pyramid. This fountain stands at the
beginning of the long avenue called the **Tapis-Vert** (Green Carpet),
at the other end of which is the great **Basin of Apollo**. In it, Tuby
depicted the god's chariot drawn by four horses emerging triumphant from the water to illuminate the sky, while the tritons
blow into their shells to announce Apollo's arrival. Behind this
sculptural group a vast area of green stretches out, interrupted by
the **Grand Canal** (62 metres wide and almost 2 kilometres long),

which is in turn met halfway along by the **Small Canal**. There are groves, pools and fountains all around: the **Dôme Grove** by Hardouin-Mansart, the **Obelisk Grove** by the same designer, the grove of the **Baths of Apollo**, the **Basin of the Putti,** adorned with sculpture done by Hardy in 1710, and the **Basin of Enceladus**, with the statue by Marsy depicting the giant who was crushed under a mountain of rocks.

THE TRIANONS – Another impressive example of the luxury of Versailles and the sumptuous life which the court led there.

GRAND TRIANON – This building was erected in a corner of the park of Versailles for Louis XIV, who used to say that the Trianon had been made for him, whereas Versailles was for the court. It was built by Mansart in 1687 in the classical forms of an Italian *palazzo*: with a single storey and large windows with Doric pilasters between them, the whole structure made from delicate pink marble. Against the architect's advice, Louis XIV also ordered the construction of the peristyle with columns and pillars which unites the two wings to the rest of the building.

Interior. The part of the building on the right includes the **Reception Suite** as well as the **Apartment of Napoleon I** (in which the royal mistresses Mme de Maintenon and Mme de Pompadour had lived previously) and the **Apartment of Louis XIV**, occupied by the king from 1703 up to his death. In the left-hand part is the **Apartment of Monseigneur**, who was the son of Louis XIV, with fine Louis XIV wood panelling.

PETIT TRIANON – Built by Gabriel for Louis XV in 1762, it is considered the palace of the royal mistresses of France. Madame de Pompadour died there in 1764 and it then became the king's favourite place for spending his free time with the Countess du Barry. Louis XVI made a symbolic gift of it to Marie-Antoinette and Napoleon gave it to his sister Pauline. With its simple façade and graceful columns, elegant style and fine proportions, the building can be considered the first example of the Neoclassical style. Inside, it retains the furniture which belonged to Marie-Antoinette.
In the garden around the Trianons, it is worth paying a visit to the small **Temple of Love**, built in 1778 by Mique, with twelve Corinthian columns and a cupola beneath which is the *statue of an adolescent Cupid*, and the **Queen's Hamlet**, a picturesque imitation rustic village with thatched cottages, a dairy, and a mill once driven by the waters of a small stream. Designed by Hubert Robert between 1783 and 1786, this was Marie-Antoinette's favourite place, where she came to spend time in the open air, pretending to be a simple country lady.

The mill of the Queen's Hamlet on the grounds of the Petit Trianon.

The Environs of Paris:
DISNEYLAND® PARIS

Easy to reach on the Métro, Disneyland® Paris is by now a 'must' for all visitors to Paris, children and adults alike. At Disneyland® Paris, with its fantastic attractions, the visitor can explore the world of fairy-tales or enjoy an adventure in space, take a ride on a steamboat or be 'shot' to the moon from a giant cannon, shudder at the holographic images of the ghosts in the haunted house or take in 3-D movies at Ciné-magique. But if that's not enough, there's always a stroll down a quiet street in an American town of the early 1900s, or a ride in the Mad Hatter's hat, or a supersonic drive through the ruins of an ancient temple.

©Disney

©Disney

Index

157

PICTURE CREDITS

The majority of the photographs in this book were taken by M. Bonechi,
S. de Leonardis, L. Di Giovine, P. Giambone, J. C. Pinheira, and A. Pistolesi
and are property of the Casa Editrice Bonechi photographic archives.

Other photographs were provided by

G. Dagli Orti: pages 5 center left and bottom, 7, 62 bottom, 74 top, 118,
120 top, 125 bottom right, 148 top.

© Photos Réunion Musées Nationaux: pages 32, 34 bottom, 35, 38 bottom, 39,
40, 41, 42, 43, 44, 45, 46, 47,48, 49, 50, 69, 71, 72, 73, 84 top right and center.

V. Gauvreau: page 86.

B. N. Cabinet des Estampes: page 6.

We would like to thank Disneyland ® Paris for their kind permission to reproduce
the photographs on page 156.

The publisher is grateful to the Press Service of the Grand Louvre for permission
to use the museum plan reproduced on page 37.